I0104671

REGAINING HUMANITY

15 Essential Character Traits to Unplug from Rule by the Elites

Scott A. Johnson

COPYRIGHT © 2021, by Scott A. Johnson

All Rights Reserved. No part of this publication may be reproduced or transmitted in any form or by any means, electronic or mechanical, including photocopying and recording, or introduced into any information storage and retrieval system without the written permission of the copyright owner. Brief quotations may be used in reviews prepared for magazines, blogs, newspapers, or broadcasts.

Regaining Humanity: 15 Essential Character Traits to Unplug from Rule by the Elites / Scott A. Johnson

ISBN-13: 978-0997548785 / ISBN-10: 0997548789

Cover design: Scott A. Johnson
Cover Copyright: © Scott A. Johnson 2021

Discover more books by Scott A. Johnson at authorscott.com

Published by Scott A. Johnson Professional Writing Services, LLC: Orem, UT

To my fellow relentless truth seekers, who vigorously seek the truth even when you must stand alone and without the support of those who should give it most. You bother to notice what is happening in the world and, more importantly, go to the trouble of finding out why. Willingly enduring the name-calling, shaming, and defaming, you genuinely strive to help others see the irrefutable facts. Just remember that Noah was considered a conspiracy theorist until the torrential rain began to fall, vindicating him as a truth spreader.

Contents

CHAPTER 1

THE HUMAN PROBLEM

Evil is not to be traced back to the individual
but to the collective behavior of humanity.

—Karl Paul Reinhold Niebuhr

As the pinnacle of creation, humans are capable of both wonderful and terrible things. Both good and evil. Indeed, people usually possess a combination of good and bad qualities. We are inherently good, endowed with a consciousness to distinguish right and wrong, but the choices we make shape and direct our lives to either maintain the path of good or depart to darker paths. There aren't good and bad people, only people who make good and bad choices.

Collectively and individually, humankind has accomplished countless amazing feats that have improved life for most everyone. The invention of printing completely changed the way information was shared and laid the groundwork for the Renaissance and the scientific revolution. It made information available to the masses that transformed the world as we know it. Since the early days, humans have dreamed of flying. The miracle of flight evolved the way people traveled and gave people the opportunity to visit distant lands, embark on adventures, and improved global commerce. The advent of computers and the internet improved information storage, simplified tasks, improved work organization, advanced business and science, and revolutionized the way we live, learn, communicate, and exchange information. A complete list of human achievements that improved the world would be nearly impossible to compile.

The remarkable thing is that even individuals can make a difference in the world. Countless individuals have left a legacy that serves as a testament to the human spirit. Doubt this? You may want to reflect on the following triumphs.

Jadav Payeng is an environmental activist who has dedicated his life to planting and tending to a forest. He has been dubbed "the Forest Man of India" because he created more than a thousand acres of forest that is now home to a variety of wildlife. His contributions have benefited animals, humans, and the planet.

Few things have impacted the world more than the invention and implementation of the internet. Tim Berners-Lee designed and built the first web browser, editor, and server in 1989, transforming the way information is created, shared, and consumed. His brilliance unleashed the World Wide Web (with help, of course), which revolutionized the world. Not satisfied with providing a platform widely used across the globe, his mission today is to increase access to the internet and save the web from political manipulation, privacy violations, censorship, and fake news.

Paul Lauterbur and Peter Mansfield won the Nobel Prize for medicine in 2003 in recognition of their invention of magnetic resonance imaging (MRI). MRI allows physicians to see inside the body's soft organs without subjecting a person to invasive surgery or X-rays. Not only does MRI enable doctors to find tumors and fractures, but also it is a highly valuable tool to gain a complete picture of soft tissue, including the brain. MRI has improved the way doctors diagnose and treat people, and saved incalculable lives.

Irena Sendler is credited for rescuing an estimated three thousand Jewish children after the Nazi invasion of Poland in 1939. The twenty-nine-year-old Polish social worker provided food and shelter to frightened Jews and even impersonated a nurse to gain access to the Warsaw Ghetto. Even after being captured and tortured by the Nazis in 1943, she refused to provide any information that would undermine the rescues. Her heroic work allowed thousands of children to grow to adulthood and have children of their own.

Nelson Mandela was a catalyst for change that led a nation, changed lives, and inspired countless individuals with his willingness to sacrifice for a worthy cause. His unrelenting actions landed him in prison for nearly thirty years, where he refused to be bullied into departing from the movement he relentlessly pursued. Standing by his fierce convictions, he brought an end to apartheid in South Africa and continued to advocate for global human rights.

No single person in human history changed the world and the lives of every person who has or will ever live more than Jesus Christ. Embracing His teachings profoundly changes the way you live. Following Him means having charity for and serving those around you. This world would be entirely different if more people chose to follow Him!

The great thing is that you don't need to change the whole world with your actions. Your actions can change your home and community. Take a meal to a neighbor in need. Shovel snow for a person who can't. Visit the elderly that are often lonely. Write a note of gratitude. Smile at total strangers. It doesn't take much to create positive effects that ripple through your community.

There is a hero, a champion, a winner inside each of us, but very few make choices that allow that hero, champion, or winner out. It could be said that many of us are living below our privilege and potential.

Unfortunately, just as individuals can positively change the world, those who choose darker paths can also terrorize and destroy other's lives.

Under the reign of Adolf Hitler, policies of Fascist Nazis—such as state-sponsored persecution—were implemented that proved ruinous. His list of brutal and horrifying atrocities includes the slaughter of millions of innocent children, women, and men and the loss of tens of millions of lives during the war he started (World War II).

Another ruthless dictator, Josef Stalin, ruled the Soviet Union by terror and caused the death of millions—by some estimates twenty million people—of his own citizens. He collaborated with Hitler by signing the German-Soviet Nonaggression Pact during World War II, making land grabs in Poland, Romania, Estonia, Latvia, Lithuania, and Finland. He was mercilessly brutal to his political enemies and dissenters, purging, executing, and exiling millions.

Mao Zedong was a ruthless Chinese communist revolutionary that converted China into a single-party socialist state. His implementation of the Great Leap Forward from 1958 to 1961 led to widespread famine in China that caused the deaths of an estimated forty- to seventy-million people, mainly because of starvation. He is also known for his systemic human rights abuses, executions, and forced labor camps.

Characterized as the most prolific female serial killer of all time, Elizabeth Báthory is estimated to have murdered six hundred people. At the beginning, she lured peasant girls to her castle by hiring them as servants and then beat and tortured them to death. Emboldened by blood lust and the ability to get away with murder, she enticed more and more victims to her castle to satisfy her bloodthirstiness, burning, starving, torturing, and mutilating hundreds of innocent girls.

A ten-year-old murderer who terrorized the United Kingdom in the 1960s, Mary Bell demonstrated a pattern of violence and an obsession with death. She strangled a four-year-old boy to death in an abandoned house the day before she turned eleven. Mary recruited her friend to help her kill and mutilate with scissors a three-year-old boy only a couple of months later. She is considered one of the youngest serial killers ever.

The term *robber baron* was coined during the late 1800s to describe a group of extremely wealthy businessmen who employed ruthless and unethical business strategies to monopolize industries vital to society. Some of the most notorious robber barons that sought riches at the expense of the lower and middle class include Cornelius Vanderbilt (transportation), John D. Rockefeller (oil), Andrew Carnegie (steel), and J. P. Morgan (steel and railroad). Their vast wealth highlighted the financial inequality of an era that unequally shifted power and wealth in favor of the ruling elites.* Morality, charity, and ethics escaped these wealthy aristocrats.

* *The term elites will be used throughout this book simply to identify the nefarious group of people involved in the secret combinations with a single term. However, it should not be construed as identifying them as better than common people. Far from it, all people have the same worth, and it is really only the elites that believe they are above others.*

In the modern era, an attempt is being made to promote moral relativism, which is a philosophy that teaches there is no absolute right or wrong, and that every individual person is entitled to decide what is right and wrong in society. Swayed by this philosophy, people believe their feelings and attitudes are central and that wrong and right is relative to the person deciding it. Morality is fundamentally removed from society in this viewpoint. It's not just that moral differences exist in divergent societies and cultures, but right and wrong are completely subjective. Yet freedom can only be maintained in a society that maintains a common sense of morality.

Moral relativism permits calling good evil and evil good because it is based on one's own opinions. It is taught as a form of tolerance for the beliefs and values of others but promotes the opposite of tolerance. Most of the time, consensus on primary moral principles is held by the majority of a culture, and only a minority of the culture dissents to choose immoral and errant ways. Moral relativism cultivates intolerance against the majority morals by a loud and vocal minority. The vocal minority wholly condemn the majority morals, believing that their version of morality should be accepted by all, and refuse to tolerate differing opinions. In other words, they take pride in a message of quality, tolerance, and acceptance, but only if that message fully conforms to their viewpoint.

Moral relativism is, in fact, a precursor to anarchy. If every man and woman is permitted to do what they think is right, how can we denounce theft, assault, slavery, or even murder? These acts considered immoral in principled society may be accepted by the individual or culture committing them and therefore can no longer be considered immoral, criminal, or punishable. Maintaining a higher moral code of right and wrong is beneficial to both individuals and society. Neal A. Maxwell said, "A society which permits anything will eventually lose everything! Therefore, recognized or not, the public has an enormous stake in private morality! Bad deeds are viewed as nobody's fault and everything as excusable on one basis or another. Amid such inversions, no wonder victims are often neglected and the guilty sometimes glorified." When people act without moral principle and common decency, self-indulgence and self-pity become the norms, and the whole of society suffers. A society of people following the principles of moral relativism lacks the character and moral clarity to thrive.

Choices have consequences. The choices each of us makes affect our paths and uniquely differentiate us from everyone else. For the most

12

part, good choices keep you heading in a positive direction. On the other hand, bad choices are counterproductive and can quickly derail you from a positive destination. Some of these decisions have long-lasting, even lifelong, repercussions. Other bad choices lead to minor detours that can be corrected with good choices.

Babies enter this world with innocent minds free from the influences of friends, institutions, school, culture, and books. Despite this, they have an inherent sense of right and wrong and the ability to make judgments about the characters of the individuals they meet. A fascinating study performed by Yale researchers in 2007 showed that infants are able to evaluate an individual's behavior toward others to determine if that person is "good" or "bad" as young as six months old.[1] Researchers staged a scene with puppets (bright shapes on a stick with wobbly eyes) that featured one puppet attempting to climb a hill unsuccessfully. The puppet struggled up the hill only to fall down repeatedly. Next, the other two puppets were introduced to either help or hinder the first puppet's progress up the hill. One puppet helped by pushing from behind, and the other puppet hindered by pushing from above. After the show, the infants were given the choice to reach for the puppets included in the activity. The infants overwhelmingly preferred the helper puppet that they perceived as supportive rather than the hindering or neutral puppet.

Despite the lack of human sounds and emotions from the puppets, the infants were able to interpret the events and the purpose of each character in the scene. In essence, the infants recognized that the puppets weren't moving at random and their actions revealed their intentions. The puppet pushing uphill was helping, so it was perceived as nice, whereas the puppet pushing downhill was perceived as mean. Similarly, adults evaluate others based on their physical appearance, words, and behaviors.

The unfortunate fact is that people can be manipulated into doing very cruel things. The notorious Milgram experiment of the 1960s showed that people are willing to inflict pain on others if they are told to do so by an authoritative figure. Researcher Stanley Milgram conducted a series of studies where participants were instructed to deliver increasingly high-voltage shocks to an actor in another room, who screamed each time a shock was delivered.[2] As the shocks became increasingly strong in power, the actor in the other room went silent. Although the shocks weren't real, the participants were made to believe they were. Shockingly, Milgram found that 65 percent of the participants were willing to deliver high-voltage shocks despite the actor's cries for help and eventual silence.

US researchers repeated this infamous experiment in 2007 and found 70 percent of people were prepared to increase the voltage delivered to the actor in the other room.[3] Participants included in the modern Milgram experiment were screened for psychiatric history, substance abuse, emotional distress, anxiety, depression, and more to exclude individuals who may be predisposed to manipulation. Participants were told they could exit the experiment at any time without any consequence. What these two experiments suggest is that humans are willing to participate in acts many would consider inappropriate or unethical because they are reluctant to confront people who abuse power.

Although not part of a publicly recognized experiment, these same tactics are unwittingly used against the public today. Authoritative figures in the form of athletes, entertainers, politicians, government employees, and those with great wealth and influence unduly influence the masses. Virtually all societies are run by elites. In the past, this was out in the open in the form of kings and queens. Today, it is less obvious which elites are controlling society, but the discerning eye and critical thinker discovers that it is extremely wealthy globalists. The common people have abdicated their power to those with the greatest affluence. Regrettably, politicians participate in the fleecing of society by pandering almost exclusively to the desires of the wealthy elites and organized groups representing large business interests.

Why is it important that we understand how the elites rule? Because failing to recognize their influence means we can't break free of their deception and manipulation. Once you gain a conscious understanding of their manipulating influence, you can unplug from certain aspects of the programming and become emancipated from psychological, emotional, physical, and spiritual enslavement.

Having a hard time believing that wealthy and powerful people form secret organizations to enrich themselves? For many, it will be difficult to comprehend and accept this notion—to unplug from the Matrix if you will—but this pattern has been used among humans from the beginning of recorded history. The Bible teaches us that Cain established what appears to be the first secret society after killing his brother Abel to get gain. The Boxers were a Chinese secret society that tried to drive foreigners out of China. Hitler leveraged secret societies to rise to power. A secret Serbian group known as the Black Hand sought to free Serbians living outside Serbia during the early twentieth century through terrorist methods, including assassinating Austrian archduke Franz Ferdinand. The Islamic-extremist terrorist group Al-Qaida is a clandestine society that still operates today. Mobs are truthfully secret societies. The Bilderberg Group hosts an annual summit that includes North American and European politicians, business leaders, financiers, and academics that allegedly plot global domination. Yale is home to the secret society called Skull and Bones that is recognized for grooming powerful members to hold powerful positions in society such as Chief Justice William Howard Taft, former presidents George H. W. Bush and George W. Bush, former Secretary of State John Kerry, associate justice to the US Supreme Court Potter Stewart, chief of CIA counterintelligence James Jesus Angleton, US Secretary of War Henry Stimson, CEO and founder of Pan Am Henry Luce, and Juan Terry Trippe, the father of mainstream media and founder/publisher of *Time*, *Life*, *Fortune*, and *Sports Illustrated* magazines.[4,5] Secret societies are all around us, infesting all levels and organizations of government and industry, and still very much flourishing.

Describing how secret combinations have caused the downfall of ancient societies, Ezra Taft Benson said, "Secret combinations are parasites that live off the spiritually dead of a society. They may not be the immediate cause of a nation's downfall, but they are the symptoms of its loathsome condition. Secret societies are formed to implement the ambitions of those who seek for power and gain. History has shown that these groups thrive in an atmosphere of conflict and social immorality. Efforts to police them or exterminate them through legislation have only forced the evil underground where it has continued to survive." Highly organized and shrewdly hidden secret combinations seeking to overthrow freedom are thriving throughout the world today and pose a significant threat to peaceful society.

To demonstrate this, one need only look at the research conducted by two university researchers, Martin Gilens and Benjamin Page.[6] They compiled data for almost two thousand proposed policy changes spanning two decades with public opinion statistics identifying whether the general public approves or disproves of the policy and how those opinions varied across income groups. The researchers separated opinions of common people (those with incomes near the fiftieth percentile) and the wealthy elites (those with incomes in the top 10 percent). They also meticulously cataloged which interest groups lobbied in support or opposition of the policies. With all the data compiled and assessed, the researchers were able to determine if common people actually get what they want as far as policy changes.

What did the researchers discover about who really rules and governs society? The ruling elites and special interest groups, of course. They concluded that "economic elites and organized groups representing business interests have substantial independent impacts on US government policy, while mass-based interest groups and average citizens have little or no independent influence." The data showed that policy makers favor policies that advance the narrow interests of the elites. At the same time, organized groups representing business push hard for positions favorable to their company and industry at the expense of the common people. Even worse, the researchers found that "when a majority of citizens disagrees with economic elites and/or with organized interests, they generally lose. Moreover, because of the strong status quo bias built into the US political system, even when fairly large majorities of Americans favor policy change, they generally do not get it." In the end, these powerful data undeniably show that the common people only get what they want if their views align with the desires of the elites.

If you are trapped in the left-versus-right paradigm when it comes to politics, you are largely missing the point. Left-versus-right ideology primarily exists to maintain the illusion of choice. If there are two choices—really, there are more than two choices, but candidates outside the two-party system are unlikely to get elected—the public can believe that one side clearly won an election. Reality is that the public gets very little actual say in who is elected. Media and huge amounts of money influence public opinion and persuade the masses to vote a certain way. At times, elections are even fraudulently manipulated to ensure an outcome favorable to the elites.

Unfortunately, this negative phenomenon will only get worse as 1) policy makers are allowed to make politics a career, 2) wealthy elites are permitted to throw their considerable wealth behind politicians and groups that will assure their interests are first and foremost, and 3) "earmarking" continues.

The term *public service* sounds like a noble endeavor, and many do enter politics with a genuine desire to positively change their communities, states, or countries. However, the longer a person is in office, the more susceptible he or she is to becoming a puppet of the wealthy elites. Those in office long enough may even begin to enrich themselves and their associates. When an individual or organization pays a large sum of money to help a politician get reelected, they expect something in return—such as policies favorable to their industry or the granting of government contracts. Similarly, a politician could potentially feed information to a friend or relative to get a government contract. For example, if businesses were bidding to build a new bridge for the government, a politician could leak information to her brother who owns a construction company so that he submits the lowest bid and thus "wins" the contract. It is far easier for the elites and business interests to maintain a relationship of control over a long-term politician instead of having to begin anew with a newly elected politician. Thomas Sowell said, "No one will ever really understand politics until they understand that politicians are not trying to solve our problems. They are trying to solve their own problems—of which getting elected and reelected are number one and number two. Whatever is number three is far behind."[7] Term limits on Congress is the best solution to this problem.

In addition, politicians tend to become more partisan the longer they remain in Congress, blaming the other side for the country's problems. Decisions of elected representatives are solely guided by what will get them reelected. Since they need great sums of money to get reelected, who do you think they favor the most? It's obvious, the people with the most money. Term limits would help prevent elected representatives from gaining too much power and becoming too distanced from the will of their constituents—we the people.

Corrupt politicians and government organizations aren't uniquely an American problem. One of the world's most respected medical journals published a condemnatory article exposing the corruption within the UK government. The article alleges that the COVID-19 pandemic was being used as a tool for political and financial gain in the mold of "some of history's worst autocrats and dictators."[8] The article found that corrupt officials failed to follow legitimate science and instead suppressed dissenting science and cherry-picked science that supported their own narratives. Essentially, the article accuses UK politicians and government of "corruption on a grand scale" and "opportunistic embezzlement," wherein they collaborated with industry to promote anticompetitive practices that favor their own business interests and those of their associates.

Those with the most affluence have the most influence in politics. The wealthy elites engage in "stealth politics," giving large sums of money to parties and politicians to advance unpopular policies that ultimately benefit their own interests. Despite how odd it sounds, the wealthy elites see themselves as a vulnerable minority because there are so few of them. As such, they seek to protect their wealth and influence by preventing strong majorities of common people from forming because they could threaten their reign of supremacy. The elites send shovels and truckloads of donations into elite institutions that brew identity politics— political party, race, sexual orientation, gender, and so on—to fragment society and prevent the formation of majorities. They convince categorized groups of people that another category of people is to blame for all their troubles. They brew hate toward people who don't look, think, and behave like their category. Hatred is such a powerful emotion that it prevents us from seeing the humanity in others. When our "enemy" lacks humanity, it is easier to commit cruel acts against them. Indeed, hatred so consumes the soul that our sole desire becomes the demise of the group our hatred is directed toward. Social and national bonds are further weakened, and divisiveness becomes the cultural norm, so the elites continue to rule the roost.

Career politicians, corrupt government agencies, contemptuous academics, entrenched bureaucrats, propagandist journalists, and highbrow corporate chiefs unite to form a military-industrial-intelligence-media complex to maintain elite control. This complex advocates for ideologies that they never suffer the firsthand consequences of. The wealthy elites have the means and influence to reduce the impact of, or avoid altogether, higher taxes and fees that come as a consequence of poorly thought-out policies. The middle- and lower-class individuals don't have the same luxury to escape increased taxes and fees. A perfect example of this hypocrisy is the stance many elites take on the environment. While the majority of ordinary people want to do what is best for the environment, green policies largely target carbon-based fuels—petroleum, natural gas, and coal—that have made up at least 80 percent of total US energy consumption for more than a hundred years.[9] One can't simply turn off 80 percent of the power grid and ask people to go on with their lives as normal. In addition, the true goal of stringent environmental policies is to transfer greater power and control to the government. It will take time to implement greener and more sustainable energy sources. While the elites scream for green policies, they themselves don't practice what they preach. They fly private jets and own multiple cars and homes while lecturing us about the environment and inequality.

Earmarking is the practice of adding provisions to congressional spending bills that fund specific projects that are championed by individual or small groups of politicians. These earmarks are much like a parasite in that they circumvent customary processes by latching on to high-priority projects that have majority support to get what they want. A perfect example of this is the $1.9 trillion coronavirus relief package passed by the US Congress. The name suggests that the spending bill was to provide relief for working-class Americans and businesses impacted by the unprecedented shutdowns to the global economy. However, over 15 percent of the bill—$300 billion—is for politician pet projects, while only about 6 percent is truly focused on resources to combat COVID-19, and nearly half is aimed at stimulus checks.[10] Politicians know that the general public wanted relief from the depressed economy that the smear politicians created, so with popularity on their side, they add earmarks that bail out poorly run states and benefit themselves.

Earmarks are also used as a vote manipulation tool. If a proposed bill fails to garner enough support to pass, congressional leaders can either rework the bill to satisfy dissenters or allow the addition of earmarks among those opposed to the bill so they get something they want in exchange for a vote. The practice of earmarking needs to end to discourage political greed, corruption, and extravagant spending.

We are told that those who don't learn from history are doomed to repeat it. Regrettably, learning from history is not always positive. Some look back at history to discover how organized secret combinations of people rose to and maintained power. This is a tactic used by the ruling elites and the complex they have formed. They have scoured history and learned from history's past controlling regimes. They have studied their methods and tactics, modernized them, and perfected the art of control.

Control the Media

Virtually every media source has a bias. The days of mainstream media (MSM) reporting the news and allowing viewers or listeners to decide what to think are over. Instead, the media attempts to tell common people what to think. Even more alarming, MSM is controlled by the ruling elites and infiltrated by corrupt government organizations. They are the communication arm of the propaganda machine controlled by the military-industrial-intelligence-media complex.

Blatant bias is recognized in many media outlets, and most often people gravitate toward media that supports their ideological preferences. AllSides Media maintains a useful list of media outlets and their biases.[11] The chart shows that media outlets like

CNN, HuffPost, and MSNBC share extremely progressive ideology; Newsmax Opinion, OAN, and The Federalist extremely conservative ideology; and BBC, Reuters, and Newsweek fall in the middle. Recognizing which media have biased ideologies allows you to consume balanced news, avoid manipulation and fake news, and gain exposure to different perspectives. The most dangerous media are those that maintain a hidden bias that misleads and divides the population.

The US Central Intelligence Agency (CIA) has had its hands in the media from its onset. The agency has recruited leading media assets, both domestic and foreign, to secretly carry out covert assignments. Student cultural organizations and magazines are funded, and journalists paid, to share CIA views. If it wasn't for the Watergate scandal, the public may have been kept in the dark about the CIA's meddling in the media for longer. During the aftermath of Watergate, Congress began questioning the CIA and uncovered the first signs of Operation Mockingbird.

Operation Mockingbird is a comprehensive CIA program with the sole purpose of manipulating the news media for propaganda purposes.[12] Beginning in 1950, the program has been used to sway public opinion and reactions to national issues with disinformation and smear campaigns. Although denied by the CIA, classified documents released in 2007 mention Operation Mockingbird a single time and reveal that two American journalists were wiretapped for several months.[13] Additionally, the CIA admitted in 1975 that they manipulate MSM and distort information to tilt the opinions of American citizens toward specific agendas.[14] In essence, MSM colludes with the CIA to sway global perception about events, people, and situations.

According to Carl Bernstein, the CIA's involvement in media continues to be shrouded in an official policy of deception and denial because it has been one of the most successful intelligence-gathering programs ever employed by the CIA. Furthermore, the

CIA continues to deny the existence because investigations would reveal humiliating relationships with powerful individuals and organizations in the media. Certainly, it would be naive to believe that this practice has been discontinued by the CIA, given its massive success.

Director of the CIA, Allen Dulles, approved the beginning of a top-secret CIA program called MK-Ultra in the 1950s. MK-Ultra was a mind-control program that employed biological and chemical materials to promote behavior modification.[15] Appallingly, human subjects—a mix of volunteers, those coerced, and people who had no idea they were being experimented on—were subjected to electroshock therapy, radiation, drugs, toxins, chemicals, and polygraphs. One of the drugs of choice was LSD (lysergic acid diethylamide) because the CIA had intercepted reports that the Soviet Union was experimenting with the drug in the 1940s. The CIA believed that LSD provided the ability to control subjects whether they were willing or not. The LSD experiments went as far as to recruit prostitutes to lure unsuspecting Johns into a room built for CIA agents to observe the actions of the Johns unwittingly dosed with LSD. The program came to an unceremonious end in 1963 when a member of the CIA inspector general's staff became aware of the project and insisted the program end.

It isn't just the American intelligence community employing disinformation and mind-control strategies. From the 1930s to the 1960s, the Soviet Union operated a system of labor camps that used imprisoned humans for mind-control experiments. It is estimated that an astonishing ten million people were held captive in the camps. During the 1960s, the Soviet Union's KGB (Komitet Gosudarstvennoy Bezopasnosti, Committee for State Security) conducted a series of psychological experiments. They discovered that barraging human subjects with fear messages nonstop brainwashed the subjects so effectively that they believed the false message. In fact, they were so brainwashed that no amount of truthful information that contradicted the implanted false message could change their minds. Carl Sagan spoke about this when he said, "One of the saddest lessons of history is this: If we've been bamboozled long enough, we tend to reject any evidence of the bamboozle. We're no longer interested in finding out the truth. The bamboozle has captured us. It's simply too painful to acknowledge, even to ourselves, that we've been taken." People today tend to be far too susceptible to being bamboozled and are dangerously disconnected from reality.

Knowing the power of swaying media, many authoritarian countries operate state-controlled media that are under financial and editorial control by the country's government. In these countries, editorial freedom is removed so that government propaganda can be pushed to the masses. Countries with state-controlled media include China, Russia, North Korea, Saudi Arabia, Vietnam, Ethiopia, Cuba, and others. Each of these countries exercises some degree of control over news networks, social media, newspapers, and radio. North Korean media is entirely state-controlled, and the government chooses all content that is published or broadcast. Russia and China provide the illusion of unbiased media by permitting a mix of state and private media, but the government still bans various content. In fact, content against the government is censored in China, and when a larger controversy goes viral on social media, these platforms are entirely shut down. Controlling the flow of information means control of the narrative and, ultimately, control of the people.

Wealthy billionaires are paying to control the media, much like governments do. Since 2003, investor George Soros has spent more than $48 million funding media, such as journalism schools and industry organizations.[16] Similarly, Bill Gates funneled massive amounts of money, through subgrants, to control the narrative surrounding the coronavirus. Media like the BBC, NPR, NBC, Al Jazeera, ProPublica, National Journal, the *Guardian*, the *New York Times*, Univision, and many more received a portion of

Gates's $250 million investment in media.[17] Amazon's Jeff Bezos decided the best approach was simply to buy the *Washington Post*. The reality is that virtually all media is controlled by some larger interest, whether by the government or wealthy individuals or a mix of both.

Create Fear

Few things are a greater motivator than fear. Fear is a primal survival mechanism that alerts us of dangers that threaten our well-being and potentially our very lives. Disregarding fear can place one in mortal jeopardy. Manipulators throughout history have learned how to establish obedient populations through fear. Truly, fear can move many people to do the oddest things, no matter how nonsensical they are. History has shown that fear, manipulated by propaganda, nearly always defeats evidence. Indeed, there is an entire school of research within public health called "fear appeal" that discovers ways to frighten people. Think back to the Milgram experiment. Subjects kept pushing a button that they believed was delivering increasingly painful shocks and may have even killed the other subject because they feared to disobey authority. Fear is the greatest weapon of tyrants and master manipulators.

Elites, and even the government, trigger fear to exploit our survival instinct. They depend on fear to secure submission, compliance, and sometimes cooperation with their endeavors. Leveraging the MSM, politicians, and others, elites inject fear into the public that sways them to causes important to maintain their power. After all, a public in a constant state of panic is easier to control.

Fear is a depreciating asset. The more fear is used to persuade the masses, the less it is believed. People are most likely to act according to a fearful warning the first time it is presented as a threat. Compliance diminishes the second time the fearful event is used and continues to decrease with each use. This is why elites must invest in their stock of fear capital—the next threat. One need look no further than how powerful fear surrounding COVID-19 has been to witness its robust effects on human behavior. COVID-19 fearmongering magnified the worst impulses of the megalomaniac elites, fueling their unsatiated desire for power, influence, and money. And most global citizens recklessly complied because they were frightened. The fearmongering worked perfectly, paving the way for the removal of wealth and freedoms from the masses, and pitting those most susceptible to the fear against those less susceptible. By maintaining a state of artificially inflated trepidation, elites prepare the masses for the implementation of measures disguised as protection from the threat that actually deprive the masses of liberty and prosperity, while enlarging the wealth and power of the elites.

It is interesting that in the 1960s and 1970s newspaper headlines warned of a cooling climate and the coming ice age. On January 30, 1961, the *New York Times* ran a story titled "Scientists Agree World is Colder," which claimed scientists unanimously agreed the world was getting colder.[18] Similarly, the January 11, 1970, edition of the *Washington Post* contained an article entitled "Colder Winters Held Dawn of New Ice Age,' where Murray Mitchell, head climatologist for the Environmental Sciences Services Administration, warned that continuing declines in global temperatures threatened to usher in the next ice age climate.[19] Papers throughout the 1970s ran similar articles that acted as fear capital to implement environmental regulations and policies. In more recent years, the fear capital has done a 180 and shifted to global warming. In 1989, a senior United Nations (UN) official predicted that "entire nations could be wiped off the face of the Earth by rising sea levels if the global warming trend is not reversed by the year 2000."[20] Back in 2009, former UK prime minister Gordon Brown said the world had only fifty days to divert climate catastrophe caused by global warming to pressure other countries to sign the Copenhagen agreement.[21] Yet here we are, decades after these failed doomsday predictions. Again, policy makers are crying for more money to be spent and regulations to be implemented to stave off a catastrophic increase in global temperatures because it is their fear capital of choice currently.

We don't necessarily face the physical threats our far-distant ancestors did, but many of the threats we do fear are the consequence of narratives fabricated by those in positions of power. If we don't recognize these fear tactics, the insane global elites will continue to manipulate us into doing their bidding.

Divide et Impera

Latin for "divide and conquer," *divide et impera* is a strategy used to usurp and preserve power by preventing the concentration of power. This political and military tactic has been used throughout history to control subjects, populations, and factions that collectively may be able to oppose the ruling class. Both the Roman and British empires pitted smaller groups of people against one another to control their territories. People are more easily controlled when they feel alone and cut off from everyone else, because if it is just you alone you are not as much of a threat. In essence, if smaller factions of people spend their time and efforts fighting each other, they will fail to unite and overthrow the true ruling power, which is weaker than the collective factions.

Flags are designed to symbolize unity and ignite pride in one's nation or organization. Yet they can also kindle significant hatred. Despite our differences, we used to rally around the flag and unite as a country, but now these very institutions and symbols are used as divisive instruments. The US military and the country have rallied around the flag at pivotal moments in history: the Battle of San Juan Hill in 1898, Iwo Jima in 1945, the moon landing in 1969, and after the World Trade Center collapse on 9/11. Similarly, people from opposing sports teams used to gather in a single sports venue to root for their team, but when the flag came out and the national anthem was sung, the crowd of opposing

27

forces united as one. Today, the flag has lost its mojo and respect among a small portion of the US population.

Discord and contention are created so that we the people are so focused on fighting among ourselves that the ruling elites easily hide the real crime scene—them plundering the very people they hoodwinked into quarreling. Nowadays, the smallest things divide people. We fight over food choices, vehicles we drive, personal health choices, a statue, labels on a food item, brand of phone, or a whole host of other seemingly insignificant issues. While absolute unity is not likely because some moral issues are too polarizing, people can find common ground on policies and priorities despite our differences. Unity is achieved when people share a common belief or vision and each individual feels acknowledged and valued. If we divide ourselves, we don't stand a chance.

Modern bridges connect two points that are divided by obstacles, such as a bodies of water, roads, or chasms deep and wide. Bridges provide passage over these obstacles that would otherwise be difficult to cross. It takes wisdom, planning, and vision to build beautiful bridges that span these gaps. Similarly, we have vast schisms fraught with raging waters separating people today. People with great courage and wisdom are needed to stand in the gap and act as a bridge to help both sides discover common ground and learn to talk to each other again. Once a bridge is built, brave men and women are needed to cross the bridge and show others the way. Finding compromise by bridging differences is urgent because the chasm between us is growing wider, to the delight of the elites, and will soon cause the fleeting bridge between us to collapse.

Some specific ideas to work toward a semblance of unity include the following:

- *Avoid derogatory terms and name-calling.* This tactic attempts to dehumanize the opposition, so we feel better when we harm them. If you can demean a person to the point you see them as no more valuable than a bug, it makes it easier to squash them without feeling remorse. The views of each person must be acknowledged and respected.

- *Seek to understand rather than assuming.* It's easy to assume a person thinks or acts a certain way rather than ask them, but this often leads to significant misunderstandings. Perhaps you are annoyed that a mother is not controlling her young children on a flight. Yet she may be struggling to control her children because she is struggling with feelings of a failed marriage and fleeing an abusive relationship. Listen to and strive to understand why someone has taken the stance they have on an issue or are behaving the way they are.

- *Exercise humility.* In some cases, you need to consider that your stance, however brilliant and well-thought-out, may not be the best one possible. Individual experiences shape our choices and beliefs, so learning from another's experience may benefit you. Often, merging parts of each person's stance leads to a better solution.

- *Agree to disagree but still show respect.* When two opposing views can't find points to agree on, agree to disagree and move on without debasing the other person. If you want your opinion respected, respect people's right to have an opinion other than yours. Thomas Sowell spoke of this when he said, "One of the most pathetic—and dangerous—signs of our times is the growing number of individuals and groups who believe that no one can possibly disagree with them for any honest reason." Too often, people attempt to vilify a person with an opposing view when they fail to convert them to their way of thinking.

Perpetual Warfare

Perpetual warfare is exploited by the ruling elite for two primary purposes: to weaken the military and economy of countries that pose a threat to their plans/rule and to generate profits. A set of banking families, united by intermarriages and blood, with deep knowledge of financial manipulation, ruthlessly control the globe partly through financing war. These powerful banking families include the Rothschilds, Rockefellers, Morgans, Warburgs, and Schiffs. An old saying declares that money makes the world go round, and wealthy bankers seek to make this true. What they realize is that he who controls the money supply controls the empires of the world. They utilize bondage debt to control governments.

Threatened by the impressive industrial growth in Germany and their lack of control over Germany's money supply, British banking and political forces united to destroy Germany as a nation during World War I. Misleading propaganda was perpetuated by the Rothschilds to mold public opinion in favor of war with Germany.[22] Reportedly, the British Treasury and finances of the British Empire were in complete disarray immediately prior to declaring war on Germany.[23] War was used as a means to rescue a nearly bankrupt country. Because of this, the bankers had all the money and therefore control of the British government. Later, these same bankers financed Nazism.

Similarly, US bankers set up foundations shielded from investigation by Congress and then filled the State Department with agents of the banking families. While the Rothschilds worked on gaining control in Britain, their allies in the United States, the Morgans, manipulated US public opinion in favor of entering the war against Germany. Congressional records from 1917 show that the Morgans held a meeting with and employed twelve influential men in the newspaper industry to control US media.[24] The entry of the United States into World War I was a preplanned scheme by the bankers so that they would be able to recover loans the Morgan's and Rothschild's banks had made to the British, Italians, and French.[25] The bankers understood that if Germany won the war—and they likely would have without US intervention—the losing countries would not be able to pay the bankers back for the loans they accumulated during the war. Woodrow Wilson, pushed into power by the bankers, was all too eager to comply and get the United States involved when he became president.

It is easy to see how entrenched bankers are in the fabric of governments when you consider the fact that banker Max Warburg was chief of German Army Intelligence during World War II. Max's brother Paul, a naturalized citizen of the United States, authored the Federal Reserve scheme. When the war ended, both brothers were delegates at the Paris Peace Conference of 1919 to ensure the interests of their banks were met. At long last, the war instigated, fueled, and prolonged by the bankers ensured them windfall profits at the expense of millions of men from twenty-one countries.

Industry also profits from war by providing things necessary to wage war: weapons, vehicles and associated parts, aircraft and associated parts, electronics, food, beverages, and more. Profiting from war even has a name—war profiteering. Although involvement in war brings death and damage, the countries involved reap economic benefits as well. A country that increases exports of necessary war supplies may decrease the amount of money they need to borrow. This was the case in the United States during the Gulf War in Iraq (August 1990 to February 1991). As a result of the Gulf War, the US decreased their deficit significantly from 1989 to 1990 ($110 billion to $99.3 billion).[26] War is currently driven by greed, power, and profit, enabled by society's fears and ignorance, and if it continues, perpetual conflict will become the norm.

Warfare was so important to officials within US government that they literally proposed the murder of US citizens. Declassified documents reveal that Operation Northwoods was a 1962 plan circulated by the Joint Chiefs of Staff to stage a false flag terrorist attack inside the United States.[27] What was the purpose of the attack? The plan was proposed to provoke public support for a military invasion of Cuba. The diabolical plot called for CIA or other operatives to commit acts of terrorism in the Miami, Florida, area, other Florida cities, and even Washington, DC, which would be blamed on communist Cuba. Without the courage of then President John F. Kennedy, who rejected the proposal twice, the operation may have been carried out. Astonishingly, the proposed plan shows just how far warmongering officials are willing to go to stage actual terrorist attacks, resulting in legitimate casualties, to sustain warfare.

War means money—at least for the ruling elites that control the industries that provide supplies related to war. War requires countries to spend lots of money to sustain war efforts, which increases national debts. Following wars, countries need to replenish capital and are therefore beholden to the ruling elite bankers for loans. The more countries that are dragged into conflict, the more national debt that is created, and the more loans wealthy bankers can profit from. Regrettably, even the deaths of soldiers lead to banker profits. According to one source, bankers profit ten thousand for every soldier that dies in battle.[28] War serves bankers, selected industries, and some countries well at the expense of our sons, daughters, husbands, wives, fathers, mothers, brothers, and sisters, who act as sacrificial pawns in the elite's bloody wars.

Welfare

Welfare is a necessary part of societies. It is intended to ensure that members of society can meet basic human needs (food, shelter, medical care, and targeted social services) when they fall on hard times. Most people will require assistance from other people at some point in their life, whether a family member, group of supportive neighbors, religious organization, community institution, or the government. This can occur from life challenges such as underemployment, job loss, or a medical challenge. Welfare plays an important role in society to help lift up and provide a basic level of well-being.

That being said, government-sponsored welfare (called the welfare state) can be a creator of destitution that perpetuates reliance on the government for basic needs as a means of control. If those who need welfare remain permanently indebted to the government, they are not likely to revolt against it. Government-run welfare largely fails because it pays people not to work and discourages them from improving their lives. One need only look at what happened when the Obama administration suspended work requirements for welfare, causing record numbers of able-bodied adults to sign up for welfare benefits to see the consequences of government reliance without expectations.[29] We need to shift our mindset from unending welfare support to short-term assistance to those in need.

Another example of how government assistance keeps people in perpetual poverty is the Natives of the American continent. The federal government appropriated control for managing Native affairs suggesting it would benefit all Natives. Government bureaucrats handle Native assets, own their lands, oversee their affairs, and insert themselves into their decision-making processes to withhold approval until a mountain of regulations is overcome. Although the US government is responsible for looking after the best interests of Natives, it has failed in its duty by all accounts.

Consequently, Natives living on reservations are among the poorest communities in the United States. An astonishing one in three Natives live in poverty, with a median income of $23,000 per year.[30] Because the federal government generally owns the land and homes of Natives—about 5 percent of Native land is privately owned[31]—they are unable to mortgage assets like other Americans. This makes it extremely difficult to acquire capital to start a business. Keeping a job is also a challenge on reservations.

According to the Bureau of Labor Statistics, Natives have the highest unemployment rates and the lowest labor force participation rates.[32] Permits for energy development on Native lands require forty-nine steps and approval from four federal agencies, compared to only four steps in the rest of America. These are just a few of the consequences of hundreds of years of government policies that have left Natives with limited economic opportunities.

One of the reasons the United States has become one of the most prosperous nations in the history of the world is protections implemented to safeguard individual liberty, private property rights, and free markets, all of which encourage innovation and entrepreneurship. Natives have not enjoyed these same protections because of federal government interference in their affairs.[33] This is the legacy of an antiquated and bigoted dogma held by federal agencies that Natives are incapable of managing their own affairs. Native entrepreneurship and innovation are substantially hindered by excess government oversight. Natives offer proof that the more the government controls the livelihood of a population, the more that population experiences never-ending poverty.

Federal interference in Native affairs under the pretense of helping them has created an endless cycle of poverty and poor opportunities. American intellectual and author William F. Buckley Jr. was absolutely right when he asserted that "there is an inverse relationship between reliance on the state and self-reliance." Overwhelming regulations and federal control of Native affairs has proven unmistakably disastrous. The key to Native prosperity is not more federal funding or oversight but in affording Natives the same freedoms the rest of America enjoys. We need to grant Natives greater tribal and individual sovereignty to jump-start wealth creation among Native communities.

Unfortunately, welfare promotes single-parent families. The system is designed to assess needs based on income, and when two parents are in the household, the benefits it provides are significantly less, if any. For instance, if a single mother earns $20,000 per year and marries the father of her child who earns the same, the couple will generally lose about $12,000 per year in welfare benefits. Single mothers are discouraged from marrying the fathers of their children because it reduces their benefits. Welfare policies have directly led to an increase in childbearing outside of marriage. Prior to the mid-1960s, the majority of children—about 93 percent—were born to married couples.[34] A steep rise in children born in single-parent households coincided with the advent of the welfare system, reaching 40.6 percent in 2013.[35] Education level also influences these statistics, with children being born in a two-parent household increasing as education level increases: 91.9 percent among college graduates, 58 percent if some college is completed, 45.5 percent if a high school graduate, and 34.8 percent among mothers who dropped out of high school.[36] The welfare system makes it economically foolish for poor mothers and fathers to marry.

Fathers have a responsibility to protect, provide, and work together with mothers to govern households. Their example of working for what you want provides hope for their children that they too can be successful if they acquire job skills and gainful employment. Without a father figure, many youth resort to criminal activity as a means to support themselves. The consequences of homes abandoned by fathers has led to increased crime and poverty.[37,38,39] Nearly three-quarters of children living in poverty reside in a home without an adult working full-time throughout the year.[40] Estimates suggest that if all current families living in poverty gained full-time employment, working at least two thousand hours per year, the child poverty rate would shrink by 72 percent. One of the greatest hurdles for these families is the prevalence of single-mother households, which further supports fatherlessness as a major limiting factor that preserves a state of poverty. Eight-five percent of youth currently in Texas prisons grew up without a father.[41] Similarly, about 70 percent of youth confined to state-operated correctional facilities in the United States—both residential treatment and detention centers—come from a fatherless home.[42] A 2009 report found that 37.1 percent of children raised in single-parent households lack self-sufficiency (defined as income above the federal poverty level and receiving welfare), compared to only 6.8 percent of children raised in a two-parent household.[43] Fatherless homes may be the single most significant social issue facing the globe today.

Welfare is serving as a substitute for a working parent making taxpayers the family breadwinner in many single-parent homes. Even when income levels are equal, children raised in a two-parent household outperform children who come from a single-parent home.[44] This suggests it is not simply poverty, but the lack of access to a father, that decreases performance and contributes to crime and poor behavior. History shows us that children raised in a two-parent home are more likely to be successful because it is frankly easier to raise them when you combine the efforts of two loving and committed adults. Fatherlessness is becoming a crisis, and welfare is contributing to that crisis. Author J. E. McCulloch perfectly portrayed the importance of a loving home and its importance to humanity when he said, "No other success can compensate for failure in the home," during the early 1900s. The humblest shack can feel immensely rich when two committed parents unitedly preside over a home filled with love and virtue.

Moreover, welfare programs discourage maintaining assets because a person must have minimal assets to be eligible for benefits. While it is reasonable to deny benefits to a couple with low income and a $1 million net worth, it makes no sense to make welfare recipients become so financially fragile to qualify for benefits. Financial fragility means welfare recipients are less able to handle a financial hardship—such as a car repair or need to replace a household appliance—in the future. Ultimately, this means the government is contributing to poverty by making it more likely welfare recipients will be hungry, unable to pay their bills, or even homeless in the future.

The goal of welfare should be to act as a temporary support until the affected individual can be empowered to take greater control of their own lives and no longer require government assistance. One of the major deficiencies of government welfare programs is the lack of emphasis on job training, education, or anything else that might allow a person to become self-sufficient in the future. A detrimental and shortsighted mindset, this keeps people perpetually dependent on government benefits. We must develop programs that enhance life and job skills and increase employability and earnings potential if we want to wean people off welfare. It is the classic story of giving a person a fish rather than teaching that person to fish. It is time to rethink the antiquated ideology that the best way to elevate people out of poverty is to expand welfare programs. Instead, the focus should be on providing means for welfare recipients to eventually become self-sufficient. Work is the fastest and most efficient way to get out of poverty. Our welfare system discourages gainful employment, dissuades families from staying together, and encourages dependency on government.

Dominate Educational Institutions

Progressive ideologies that facilitate the ruling elite's control have dominated the school system for decades. Ideological agendas are taught over serious learning in many schools across the world. Parents have little visibility into what is taught in public, and sometimes private, schools, making it easy for educators to introduce controversial curriculum unnoticed. This lack of transparency leads to dangerous and indoctrinating curriculum being force-fed to impressionable children.

Don't believe it? Some school English classes have adopted the book *Symptoms of Being Human* (a novel about a gender-fluid punk rocker) as required reading. At the same time, well-known classic novels like *To Kill a Mockingbird*, *Of Mice and Men*, and *The Adventures of Huckleberry Finn* are banned because a minority of parents are offended by their purported racial undertones. Despite a handful of racial slurs, *To Kill a Mockingbird* is not a racist book; quite the contrary, the book takes a sympathetic view of minorities and explicitly condemns racism, while simultaneously preaching acceptance and fairness. Good books produce good readers, and the classics have the potential to cultivate a love of reading that cannot be matched by the likes of the current attempt to encourage social-justice young-adult fiction. Modern students are taught to hate the very country that tens of thousands of individuals seek to enter illegally each year, the United States. Howard Zinn's anti-American interpretations of history are woven into social studies in both high school and college classes. His book *A People's History of the United States* teaches that America is founded on a litany of oppression, slavery, and exploitation.[45] Public schools in Chicago adopted American history curriculum based on the 1619 Project, which teaches that the United States was not founded by the Declaration of Independence but by the arrival of the first slaves in Jamestown in 1619.[46] This widely refuted maligning of the United States perpetuated by the *New York Times* teaches young children that the United States is fundamentally racist and white Americans are responsible for all current and past racism. This despite the fact that slavery has existed among virtually all cultures and peoples throughout history. Math becomes a social justice initiative rather than a means to develop reasoning and analytical thinking. Seattle public schools implemented a K-12 math ethnic studies framework in 2019 that is laced with social justice jargon completely unrelated to math and essentially teaches that math is oppressive to people of certain ethnic backgrounds.[47] Liberal college professor, Laurie Rubel, of Brooklyn College even went as far as to claim in a tweet that $2 + 2 = 4$ "reeks of white supremacy." Fringe groups perpetuate that math is too focused on getting the right answer and that teaching that math always has a right and wrong answer creates fear of open conflict. Modern math is being transformed into "ethnomathematics," where correct answers depend on your ethnicity. Advocates of ethnomathematics are actually harming the very groups of students they claim to be trying to help by denying them the opportunity to learn the precise mathematics required for careers in engineering, aerospace, physics, and other sciences. Concepts of gender identity and sexual orientation are becoming normal in sex education classes. The California Department of Education approved controversial sex education guidelines for public schools in 2019. The curriculum encourages teachers to discuss gender identity with kindergartners, LGBT relationships with teens, and give masturbation tips to middle-schoolers.[48] Sexual feelings are normal and expected as children mature, but they shouldn't be taught to act on sexual feelings whenever and however they want to. Parents have the primary responsibility to teach children about their sexual intimacy honestly and plainly at age-appropriate times. It is not the responsibility, nor the right, of schools to teach progressive views of sexuality that don't align with parental beliefs. Parents around the world are waking up to the reality that their children are being subjected to sexual indoctrination in the form of sex education. Indeed, extremist sex education could be considered preparatory material to groom children for sexual exploitation. Divisive identity politics infiltrate impressionable minds. Cambridge public schools in Massachusetts and schools in Southington, Connecticut, teach of the hazards of "whiteness" and forms of "white privilege."[49,50] Cases of school children, as young as elementary-aged, being taught critical race theory have become increasingly common in recent years, which further categorizes and divides people against each other. These are just a few examples of the questionable curriculum your children are being taught, most likely without your knowledge. Essentially, children are being taught that the past is horrifying, sexual identity is adaptable, merits are largely based on skin color rather than character, and they have no future.

Radical reforms and distorted ideology have metastasized throughout public education to brainwash children to think a certain way. What does this provocative curriculum, textbooks, teachers, and ideologies lead to? Confusion, division, and separation. It is ironic that an institution such as public education can teach children knowledge and skills that lead to success but at the same time can destroy lives and futures. Political correctness and identity politics have infested institutions of learning from elementary through college, and it all benefits the elites and their ability to maintain rule.

Tax Policy

Money is power and the ruling elites know this. Therefore, they donate significant money to organizations and politicians that influence tax policy favorably for their own interests. The leak of the Panama Papers—11.5 million encrypted confidential documents from Panamanian law firm Mossack Fonesca containing the tax-evasion methods of multiple wealthy individuals and public officials—prove the ruling elite have established a rogue system of international agreements, corporate cutouts, and legal loopholes to evade taxes and stockpile massive amounts of wealth.[51] These telling documents expose how elites, including wealthy individuals, celebrities, public officials, and business people, use a network of tax havens to commit fraud, dodge tax obligations, and avoid international sanctions.

According to the papers, law firms like Mossack Fonesca exist to facilitate the network and assist wealthy elites through complex policies and establish shields from accountability to profit off the plundering of society. In collaboration with law firms, politicians act as protectors of this corrupt system as they themselves become beneficiaries. They pass laws and implement policies that hide the corruption in exchange for kickbacks from the moneyed elites. Allegedly, the wealthy elites have donated billions in legal contributions to global political races, employed thousands of lobbyists to do their bidding, paid bribes, and engaged fixers to protect their racketeering system. The largest beneficiaries of this system are the ruling elites who buy power and influence to protect their interests. Ignorance is bliss, and the less the public knows of this system, the more efficiently it continues. A self-perpetuating mechanism of exploitation and greed enriches all involved parties to the detriment of all who are outside the system.

Entertainment

Once you understand the concept of the ruling elites, you'll see that they flaunt their controlling tactics throughout entertainment, particularly movies and television. Within shows—once appropriately called *programs*—the ruling elites portray and divulge the methods they use to maintain power and control in plain sight. Why do they do this if it may reveal their secretive ways? Because portraying their methods in a fictional story makes it remain an imaginary tale rather than reality in the minds of the watchers. While there may be a few within entertainment that expose these tactics in genuine efforts to warn the public, most of it is done to flaunt their unchecked strategies. If you watch movies and television with an eye for this, you will see that it is far more rampant than you probably realize. Hints of media manipulation, false flag operations, wealthy backers manipulating global issues, and more are infused in the stories contained within movies and television shows. Watching endless entertainment is designed to affect our behavior and desensitize us when people treat each other terribly.

Some contend that the CIA has shifted to or added Hollywood as a partner to manufacture truth and shape public opinion. During the 1990s, the agency built relationships with the entertainment industry to create a more favorable view of the agency and its agents in movies and television. This included hiring Chase Brandon (a veteran clandestine agent) to work directly with screenwriters, directors, and producers to upgrade the CIA's image.[52] Thus cemented the propagandist relationship between Hollywood and Langley.

In addition, Judicial Watch released a 2012 CIA inspector general's audit that exposed cooperation between the CIA and the entertainment industry.[53] Specifically, the report criticizes public affairs officials in the CIA for inviting entertainment industry workers to secret CIA briefings and other events—even those discussing classified information.

Covert collaborations between intelligence agencies and entertainment workers have been going on for quite some time. Hollywood players have been recruited for various covert intelligence operations. Billionaire film producer Arnon Milchan obtained sensitive technical information regarding defense programs for Israeli intelligence.[54] Milchan even implicated Academy Award–winning director Sydney Pollack as another operative recruited by the intelligence community.[55] According to John Rizzo in his book *Company Man: Thirty Years of Controversy and Crisis in the CIA*, the CIA has formed a special relationship with the entertainment industry, recruiting studio executives, producers, directors, and big-name actors to give more visibility and credibility to CIA propaganda projects. Likewise, Dr. Matthew Alford argues in his book *Reel Power: Hollywood Cinema and American Supremacy* that the US Department of Defense, FBI, and CIA have collaborated with the entertainment industry since 1911 in exchange for control over the content of hundreds of films. Their book is based on thousands of documents acquired through the Freedom of Information Act that outline these interactions. Altogether, evidence is growing that government agencies are aggressively collaborating with the entertainment industry to modify, censor, and manipulate films and television.

Even if you look past much of the vulgar, violent, derogatory, and inflammatory lyrics in the music industry, it is hard to miss the use of odd or cryptic symbolism by popular artists. It is found in music videos, album covers, and even in the clothing and jewelry they wear. Pentagrams, all-seeing eyes, upside-down crosses, and making devil horns with fingers each deliver hidden meanings known only to a small group of people. For example, the all-seeing eye found abundantly in the industry—music videos, photo shoots, performances, making a triangle shape with hands—reportedly represents the secret societies and sinister conspiracies of the elites. Are these musicians spreading occult ideologies, declaring allegiance to the ruling elites, revealing dastardly but hidden exploits, seeking to establish their own religion where they are worshipped by fans, or something else? If any of this is indeed true, the entertainment industry at large adds to the powerful propaganda arm of the ruling elites and their industry-government complex.

Social Media

The goal of social media is to keep you occupied on it for as long as possible so you can be sold to advertisers more frequently. You are literally the commodity on most social networks, being sold to the highest bidder. And it's not just advertisers of products and services you are being sold to. Social media is also used as a tool to shape perception and influence the behavior and governance of the people who consume it.[56] Ironically, social media was once seen as a way to liberate people from the propagandist MSM controlled by elitist oligarchs. Today, social media is controlled by these same oligarchs who use it as a platform to push horrific propaganda and spread disinformation that angers and divides the people.

Social media propaganda seems to be more effective in painting a specific narrative than MSM. It has long been used to influence, distract, persuade, and divide audiences. For example, under Vladimir Putin, Russia initiated a disinformation campaign that painted Ukraine as a corrupt, fascist state with anti-Semitic views.

That impression of Ukraine has been preserved among European and American citizens even though Ukraine elected a Jewish president. In reality, Russia was attempting to subvert Ukraine from further tilting West after the pro-Russian president of Ukraine was deposed in 2014. This clearly demonstrates that propagandistic messages sponsored by state actors can change public opinion and stimulate political rhetoric against specific targets.

Similarly, China preys on US social media platform members to perpetuate propaganda. While the Chinese Communist Party's (CCP) control over Chinese social media networks is acknowledged, some may be surprised how much money the CCP spends to manipulate messages in the United States as well. China has invested heavily in an extensive communication apparatus on Facebook since 2013 that gives them access to more than 100 million followers.[57] During 2020, the CCP went to great efforts to manipulate the narrative surrounding the SARS-CoV-2 virus. They intentionally spread disinformation to hide the chaotic early stages of the virus's spread in China even as brave Chinese citizens and scientists shared numerous details contradicting the official state narrative.

Avram Noam Chomsky, an American linguist, cognitive scientist, and social critic, reportedly warned that media creates artificial wants, division among people, and turns people into "isolated atoms of consumption, obedient, having the 'right' opinions which don't bother [elites]." Social media practices mind manipulation to manufacture compliance, and modern technology makes it so much easier to make false news appear factual. Photoshopped pictures, altered or deepfake videos, modified news headlines, and adjusted social media posts all parade on social media outlets as the truth.

Instead of stifling disinformation, more and more governments controlled by the elites are leveraging social media to influence public opinion by placing their own propaganda on the platforms. Lies are paraded as truth. Booker T. Washington rightly warned that "a lie doesn't become truth, wrong doesn't become right, and evil doesn't become good, just because it's accepted by a majority." At the core of it all are the ruling elites who act as the primary news fabricators and whose opinions populate a significant portion of information disseminated on social media. They don't care about building a better society; they are solely focused on control.

At this pivotal time in history, an awakening among the general population must occur. A well-informed population skilled in critical thinking is the elite's worst enemy. Awareness of the manipulation is the first step to changing the collective consciousness and potentially transform the globe. We, as a global people, need to decide if we will sit back in obedience and let the ruling elite win by rigging the system, or if we will have courage and take our communities back. The imperative questions are, what do we do to break this cycle of control? How can we break free of being a pawn in the ruling elite's game? How can we come together and emphasize respect over conflict and division? And finally, what can we do to regain humanity?

The bottom line is that, as humans, we all bleed the same. Underneath our differently toned skin, we are all very similar, with beating hearts, blood vessels, and more. Despite our outward differences, we are all connected. Life is not about individuals; it is about humanity as a whole. We need to rise above the current culture of "us versus them" that personifies the hateful rhetoric that something is wrong with you if you don't look, act, and think like me. A new paradigm must replace this archaic thinking. One that embraces diversity and seeks to find issues we do and can connect on. We won't agree on everything, and that is okay. However, there is plenty to agree on and causes to champion together. If each of us made a conscious choice to find connection with others, world culture would tilt in a positive direction.

Directional change does not happen overnight, but even the longest journey is completed one step at a time. Each connection we forge is a step toward a culture of inclusion and love.

Regaining humanity requires fostering characteristics that enhance connections, increase understanding and kindness towards other people, and allow the best in each of us to emerge. Fifteen of the most essential character traits to live a happier life also empower us to reclaim humanity from the grips of societal elites. These character traits are fundamental to human existence. They will impact your life and others in a positive and lasting way. Each trait developed cuts another manipulation cord of the puppet master elites cleverly engineered to bind your mind, body, emotions, and spirit. Improve your life by implementing them and inspire the next generation to regain humanity.

> I hope that people will finally come to realize that there is only one "race"—the human race—and that we are all members of it.
>
> —Margaret Atwood

CHAPTER 2

CRITICAL THINKING

The function of education is to teach one to think intensively and to think critically. Intelligence plus character—that is the goal of true education.

—Dr. Martin Luther King Jr.

Critical thinking is the ability to skillfully think and reason as you evaluate ideas and make judgments. It is an intellectually disciplined process that guides belief and action through integrating experience, knowledge, observation, and reasoning. Concisely, it combines knowledge with what you have seen, heard, and experienced, so you can make a rational and reasonable conclusion. Critical thinking attempts to analyze and assess, at the highest level and in a fair-minded way, the validity of something. It cannot adequately be performed without carefully and systematically scrutinizing and comparing several possible answers to the question at hand. It almost acts as a check-and-balance system because it allows you to recognize the strengths and weaknesses of a conclusion and reshape it into an improved form.

Thinking about your own thinking is called metacognition. More precisely, metacognition allows you to monitor and control cognitive processing to manage behavior in a way that helps you achieve your future goals. By improving the way you think and being more aware of how your thinking affects your behavior, you achieve better outcomes. Metacognition involves an awareness of your own knowledge (both what you do and don't know) and self-reflection on your current position and future goals. Successful individuals have learned this skill and have a greater capacity to regulate their cognitive processes.[58] Metacognition is an important component of everyday life and critical for successful lifelong learning. It enables you to quality-control your thinking and then modify both your thinking and behavior to improve the possibility of goal achievement.

The most difficult aspect of critical thinking is to disconnect from previously established opinions and feelings about a situation or subject. Failing to do so can result in cognitive dissonance—a conflict of two opposing attitudes, beliefs, or behaviors that results in mental discomfort. Cognitive dissonance causes people to either act in a manner contradictory to their beliefs or to adapt their beliefs to align with their actions. In neither situation do you remain authentic. Facts and truths are unbiased and cannot be swayed to one side or another based on feelings. Despite this, many people establish "truths" in their minds that are solely based on their feelings. In essence, we reinforce and justify our decisions to reduce any mental discomfort felt regarding our decision between the two opposing choices.

This concept may be easiest to understand with an example. Let's say you want a new car. You evaluate all your options and narrow it down to two equally good options (car A and car B). Finally, you choose car A. Your decision has now been made, and so your positive feelings toward car A amplify, and your negative feelings toward car B increase. Why is this happening when each car choice was initially equal? Because otherwise, your choice wouldn't make sense. Car B needs to look worse than car A to justify your decision. In its most basic form, cognitive dissonance is a lie to oneself.

A real-world example thoroughly portrays this flawed thinking. After the horrific mass shooting that took the lives of ten people in Boulder, Colorado, on March 21, 2021, social media was full of individuals parading their conclusions about what happened without any evidence. These individuals didn't wait for any facts before making assumptions that support their feelings on issues. Nor did they express concern for the victims and their families. They went straight to weaponizing the incident to advance causes they value and further spread their narrow, but entrenched, beliefs of the world.

Individuals who see racism in everything loudly expressed that the shooter was a white supremacist. People who believe that law enforcement secretly want to kill people of color claimed that the shooter must be white because he was captured alive. Some even boasted that they would bet large sums of money that the shooter was a right-wing Donald Trump supporter and white male. Others who yearn for very strict gun laws renewed calls to ban various guns and gun magazines, choosing to assign blame for the tragedy to the inanimate gun and not the wielder of the gun. Misguided individuals epitomized placing feelings over facts and capitalizing on misfortune.

However, their narrative came crashing down hard when it was revealed that the shooter was a twenty-one-year-old Muslim immigrant from Syria. Further scrutiny revealed that the shooter's social media was riddled with posts expressing hatred for former president Donald Trump and his administration's immigration policies. So the shooter was not white, a white supremacist, or a Trump supporter; neither did police capture him alive because he was white. As far as those calling for stricter gun laws, these individuals fail to realize that people who want to commit crimes will find ways to get guns. Killers don't obey gun-control laws. Boulder already had very strict gun laws—red-flag laws, universal background checks, high-capacity magazine ban, city ban on "assault weapons," and gun-free zones—and the laws didn't deter the shooter at all. Stricter gun laws only limits access to law-abiding citizens. Don't think so? Just look at what happened during the prohibition of alcohol. It didn't meaningfully reduce alcohol consumption and distribution. The mob and other enterprising individuals created speakeasys and profited off the underground sale of alcohol. The Boulder shooting demonstrates that people make poor assumptions based on what they wish to see and neglect to show compassion towards the victims of the crime, which happened to all be white.

Author and psychologist Dr. Carole Wade identified eight characteristics of critical thinking:[59]

Asking questions. This is the fact-finding and information-gathering portion of critical thinking. In this stage, we need to ask interrogative questions to discern truth. To learn more, we ask who, what, why, where, when, and everything else we can to make sense of a situation of concept. Don't take everything at face value when gathering answers to your questions. We should be skeptical of authoritarian figures who tell us to believe something is true. If what they say is true can't stand the scrutiny of skepticism, it probably isn't really true. Ask who is going to profit from a belief in this claim. Why would someone want me to believe this claim? Don't be afraid to ask probing and difficult questions and evaluate all angles of an argument. It is impossible to be a mediocre questioner and critical thinker because questions drive thinking forward. If you ask trivial rather than deep questions, you can expect trivial answers. Critical thinkers ask questions central to the issue at hand, which spark additional questions, until they are satisfied that they have gathered enough information.

Defining a problem. "If I were given one hour to save the planet, I would spend fifty-nine minutes defining the problem and one minute resolving it," Albert Einstein famously said. While it may seem extreme, the importance of clearly defining a problem can't be overstated. Failing to do so makes your solution imprecise, or answer incompletely resolved. You may also miss opportunities, waste resources, and pursue a nonproductive path. Well-defined problems lead to simpler, more complete, and more effective solutions. Critical thinkers take adequate time to define unambiguous solutions.

Examining evidence. Once you have gathered information supporting a particular argument, your next step is to examine the evidence in support of the claim. Evaluating evidence is a necessary part of the decision-making process. False "evidence" masquerading as truth is rampant in today's society. Virtually anyone can create supportive materials and post them online to portray a subject in a specific way whether the materials are factual or not. The sufficiency, credibility, and accuracy of the evidence must be determined. Is there enough evidence from credible sources, and has the claim in the argument been accurately portrayed based on the evidence? Critical thinkers seek appropriate and credible information from trustworthy individuals and sources rather than relying on obscure and anonymous sources.

Analyzing assumptions and biases. This is critical to avoid cognitive dissonance. We need to assess our own biases and assumptions because it is human nature to want to see and hear things that support our preconceived notions and be repelled when information contradicts these notions. Biases and assumptions cloud judgment and stifle forward thinking because we assume certain ideas or facts are invalid to maintain the status quo. As hard as it may be, ideas that oppose our assumptions and biases require careful consideration. We may find out that our assumptions and biases were indeed nonfactual, and confronting them can help us adjust to new, more meaningful and accurate perspectives. Critical thinkers bring awareness to their own biases and assumptions and strive to limit the impact they have on their thinking.

Avoiding emotional reasoning. Emotional reasoning is a cognitive process where your emotional response decides what is true despite evidence to the contrary. The hazard of this type of faulty thinking is that our feelings overrule facts. Instead of critical thinking (including logic, reason, and careful thought), we let our emotions (e.g., anger, jealousy, resentment, elation, and joy) decide truths. Feelings and emotions become paramount at the expense of objective and rational facts, triggering a blatant denial and rejection of reality. Today, more than ever, people tend to shape reality based on their emotions, deliberately ignoring irrefutable facts. Critical thinkers separate their emotional response from the truth and reevaluate distorted thoughts before they become strong emotions that warp reality.

Avoiding oversimplification. Oversimplification reduces the complexity of a problem so severely that it distorts reality. Complex issues have many layers that must be addressed before a viable solution is found. Too often, issues are oversimplified so that only a single solution can be presented to change the situation. Protection from the SARS-CoV-2 virus is a great example of oversimplification. The oversimplified solution for the virus and its subsequent illness became an experimental vaccine (some would argue that it was an mRNA biologic, not a vaccine). One could argue that a secondary oversimplified solution was mask wearing. The reality is that the virus's success and ability to infect people depends on a multiplicity of factors that influence health and immune function, including nutrition, hydration, exercise, sleep, stress and emotional management, exposure to toxins, supplementation, handwashing, staying home when sick, informed self-care, and proactive medical care. Focusing only on a vaccine solution is oversimplification of a complex process.

The same oversimplification occurs in politics. Many are concerned with income equality—the difference in wealth among the rich and poor—and quick to assign blame strictly to greedy corporations that use a variety of methods to gain an edge in society. However, this limited view of the issue fails to recognize the role of other factors. Government officials accept bribes and kowtow to aggressive lobbyists who demand policies favorable to large corporations. People spend large amounts of money with

52

these megacorporations, bolstering profits and consenting to their unethical practices. Automation technology replaces many workers at factories, grocery stores, and fast-food restaurants. Low-income earners lack access to training and education opportunities to increase their skills and become more employable in higher-paying jobs. These are just a few of the factors that contribute to income equality, and a critical thinker recognizes that each needs to be addressed to enact change.

Oversimplification allows individuals to pursue the path of least resistance, but it also means a less desirable outcome. It really is a lazy solution for complex issues. Critical thinkers recognize that virtually all problems and situations are multilayered and demand comprehensive solutions to solve and improve them.

Considering other interpretations. Before finalizing your conclusion, examine it carefully and consider if there are additional explanations for the problem or situation being considered. There may be more than one interpretation to your initial conclusion. Exercise caution before drawing premature conclusions rather than accepting the first good idea that comes to mind. Critical thinkers reflect on as many reasons as possible before the best one is selected as "the" conclusion.

Tolerating ambiguity. Sometimes, there is insufficient evidence, or the answer is too uncertain, to draw a definitive conclusion. Tolerance of uncertainty has even been associated with creativity because creative people find ambiguous situations interesting.[60] On the other hand, people intolerant to ambiguity feel stressed, nervous, and irritated. Accept a tentative conclusion until additional information can be collected to come to a better solution. Critical thinkers accept, if not embrace, ambiguity to generate divergent ideas.

NASA (the National Aeronautics and Space Administration) teaches a three-day course on the five types of critical thinking that can be used at NASA: strategic, tactical, analytical, innovative, and implicative. They do so to teach their employees how to employ divergent thinking approaches to solve complex problems, maximize results, and achieve mission success. Space travel involves significant unknowns and challenges that are impossible to predict. Critical thinking makes better NASA employees and improves the safety and performance of astronauts.

Thus was the case with the Apollo 13 mission. Designed to be NASA's third moon-landing mission, an unforeseen vessel failure pivoted the mission to a rescue attempt. An oxygen tank exploded as the three-man crew approached the moon, forcing the abandonment of the moon landing. Astronauts Jim Lovell, Fred Haise, and Jack Swigert deserted the command module for the small lunar module—similar in size to the interior of a VW Beetle. Unfortunately, the lunar module wasn't designed to be used for a long period, only as transportation from the command module to the moon and back. It contained only enough oxygen for two astronauts for thirty-six hours, not three astronauts for ninety-six hours. Not only was the mission a failure, but also it threatened the lives of three men.

For four days, the brave astronauts fought to stay alive in the cold vacuum of space in tight quarters. Meanwhile, NASA engineers, pilots, and flight controllers rapidly sought a solution to the problem. Fortunately, NASA had employed advanced design thinking, where they assess known problems as well as uncertain factors that may contribute to a problem. They had employed the *defining the problem* aspect of critical thinking to ensure mission success.

In a desperate move to save the lives of the astronauts, NASA employees on the ground spliced together a makeshift adapter using only items available in the lunar module to get the CO_2 scrubbers (equipment that absorbs carbon dioxide) to work overtime. Everything from duct tape to socks was used in the plan communicated to the crew in space. Thanks to the NASA brain trust and critical thinking, the three astronauts safely splashed down to Earth four days after the unexpected explosion. Lessons learned from the mission permitted the continued success of NASA's next four missions to the moon.

The ruling class doesn't want you to think for yourself. They want you to be obedient and follow their playbook. They don't fear individuals, compliant or resistant. They fear people uniting behind causes and talking about situations outside the playbook. Resistant individuals are only feared by elites when they begin uniting enough people to overthrow them. Elites attempt to overwhelm the public with nonsense and false narratives that maintain the present circumstances. Only when enough people rise above this tactic of befuddlement and control through critical-thinking skills will their rule be threatened.

There is a general lack of critical-thinking skills today. Each of us, regardless of socioeconomic circumstances or education level, has the ability to think critically. Critical thinking can also be developed. Adding it as part of the core curriculum in schools will increase equitable opportunities—socioeconomic, academic, government—throughout society. Students can be taught to observe what happens around them, remain objective in their evaluations, listen actively, and communicate effectively. Young people will therefore be endowed with creativity and the ability to think outside the box to help manifest a reality outside the paradigm of the ruling elite.

> It is the mark of an educated mind to be able
> to entertain a thought without accepting it.
>
> —Aristotle

CHAPTER 3

GRATITUDE

> It's a funny thing about life, once you begin to take note of the things you are grateful for, you begin to lose sight of the things that you lack.
>
> —Germany Kent

An attitude of gratitude is one of the most profound states of mind a person can strive for. Simply defined, gratitude is an intentional appreciation for what you have and a purposeful recognition for what others have done for you. By practicing gratitude daily, you become more aware of your blessings and what makes you a happier person. Gratitude is restorative to the soul.

Science has discovered a multitude of powerful emotional, physical, and spiritual benefits of gratitude. It's not surprising that gratitude improves emotional balance. Indeed, gratitude decreases toxic emotions like anger, regret, and envy and replaces them with calmness, contentment, and happiness. Gratitude's emotional benefits are founded in neuroscience. Researchers discovered that practicing gratitude changes the molecular structure of your brain. It helps maintain healthy brain gray-matter function.[61] Brain gray matter contains the largest collection of neuronal cell bodies and is involved in memory, emotions, intelligence, sensory perception, decision-making, and self-control. Since healthy brain gray matter is associated with better cognitive performance, you can literally make your brain function better by expressing gratitude regularly. Additionally, functional magnetic resonance imaging (fMRI) shows that gratitude synchronizes the activation of multiple brain regions and stimulates parts of the brain associated with reward and emotions.[62] Apparently, gratitude is not only life changing but brain changing.

Grateful people tend to experience more positive emotions and traits—warmth, friendliness, openness to feelings, patience, and assertiveness—and less negative emotions and traits—anger, hostility, emotional vulnerability, sadness, anxiety, self-consciousness, and impulsiveness.[63,64,65] A general pattern among research indicates that gratitude amplifies adaptive personality traits that improve overall well-being and help us maintain positive relationships. Negative emotions are part of the human experience, but life is better when we spend more time experiencing positive emotions, which can be generated by gratitude.

Gratitude is also positively associated with increased joy in life among young children, adolescents, and teens. A recent study found that gratitude is directly linked to happiness in children by age five.[66] This suggests that teaching your children to be grateful and express gratitude regularly could help them become happier teens and adults. Positive associations between gratitude and life satisfaction, optimism, social support, and more social behavior were also reported in a study of adolescents (aged eleven to thirteen).[67] Adolescents that expressed gratitude were more likely to feel hopeful, inspired, excited, and even forgiving. Similarly, grateful teens are more satisfied with their lives, are more engaged in hobbies and schoolwork, and get better grades in school.[68] Moreover, the research found that grateful teens are less envious, depressed, and materialistic when compared to less grateful teens. Clearly, there are many reasons to help children establish a pattern of gratitude early in life. It doesn't hurt that you are likely to be more pleasant to be around if you practice gratitude.

Gratitude can improve relationships—with a spouse, child, parent, sibling, colleague, teacher, and so on—and the trust within these relationships. It is most deeply felt when it arises from a genuine place. All too often people dismiss gratitude as a sentimental, unnecessary, or empty gesture in relationships. They may do so because they feel their gratitude is understood and doesn't require verbalizing or showing in another way. Nevertheless, humans have an innate desire to be appreciated and to be recognized for the value they add to other's lives. Failing to express gratitude may leave the other party in an important relationship feeling taken for granted.

Feeling gratitude in a relationship helps us identify people who are responsive to our needs, which inevitably causes us to grow closer to them. Gratitude motivates reciprocal behavior in relationships (both parties are more attentive to the other's needs), which in turn increases feelings of gratitude so that both people in the relationship gain greater gratitude.[69] Being grateful increases trust in relationships.[70] Trust is important because it is essential for career, government, and social systems.

All couples experience conflict in their relationship. This can occur for a variety of reasons and often challenges the couple's resolve and commitment to one another. A study from the University of Georgia suggests that a little bit of gratitude can protect marriages during times of conflict. The researchers conducted 468 phone interviews with married participants to evaluate to what degree they felt valued by their spouse, their financial burdens, and the frequency to which conflict caused one of the spouses to withdraw from a conversation.[71] They also asked probing questions to assess the couple's current marriage quality. Remarkably, the research found that gratitude was the most important predictor of marital quality regardless of the level of conflict within the marriage.

Gratitude can also contribute to improved interpersonal relationships among classmates. Researchers evaluated this concept among college sorority sisters. Older sorority sisters were instructed to give a gift to newer members during one week of the school year. What the researchers observed was that new sorority sisters who expressed more gratitude for their gifts developed a deeper relationship with the one that gave them the gift.[72] It is clear that expressing gratitude helps you feel more positive toward people you have relationships with.

The benefits of gratitude are not isolated to emotional and mental well-being. Research has just begun to investigate how gratitude influences physical health as well, but what has been discovered thus far is promising. This is no surprise when you look at health holistically and consider all aspects of well-being: physical, emotional, mental, and spiritual. When any area of well-being is improved or decreased, the other areas are bound to be affected in some way.

Interestingly, researchers found that gratitude helps reduce life's aches and pains. Sometimes, it is difficult to feel thankful when you're living with constant, or even temporary, pain. But gratitude seems to redirect your thoughts away from pain and provides a more positive focus. College students participated in a study where their responses to pain stimulation were evaluated in two separate experiments: behavioral and brain responses (fMRI).[73] The experiments were designed so that a participant received a painful stimulation that could be shared by a partner or not. Shared pain meant that both the participant and the partner felt less pain. If the pain was not shared, the participant took the full brunt of the pain alone. Sometimes, the partner intentionally chose to share the pain, and at other times, the partner was forced to share the pain based on a computer algorithm. The researchers found that the participants' gratitude increased when the pain was intentionally shared, and this led to a lower perceived pain intensity. This experiment shows that intention matters. When we are willingly helped by another person, we experience greater gratitude than when a person is forced to help us.

Gratitude promotes restful sleep. An attitude of gratitude shifts your thoughts from worry (something that often keeps people up at night) to the good things in your life. Researchers at the University of California, Davis conducted three experiments in the early 2000s to determine how gratitude affects perceived well-being.[74] During experiments one and two, participants were randomly assigned to one of three groups: 1) documenting hassles, 2) listing things they were grateful for, or 3) recording neutral life events or social comparisons. The journals were kept weekly in experiment one and daily in experiment two. In the third study, people with neuromuscular disorders—a group of people known for disrupted sleep—were assigned to a gratitude or control group. In all three experiments, the grateful groups exhibited heightened well-being across most of the outcome measures. Not only did the people with neuromuscular disorders experience improved well-being, but also they reported getting longer, more refreshing sleep. The research demonstrates that a positive focus on blessings provides emotional and interpersonal benefits, which can include improved sleep.

Years later, another group of researchers in England assessed how gratitude affects sleep. The study included more than four hundred adults, 40 percent of which who had a sleep disorder.[75] Participants completed questionnaires that included gratefulness, sleep quality, presleep thoughts, personality traits, and personal attributes. Gratitude was associated with an increase in positive thoughts and fewer negative thoughts at bedtime, and in turn, falling asleep faster and improved sleep duration and quality. Another study also reported that gratitude quiets the mind to help university students sleep better.[76]An attitude of gratitude seems to shift one's focus to a more tranquil state that allows for improved sleep.

Cardiac coherence is a state of harmony wherein our breathing and heart rhythms are synchronized. When a person achieves this state, major body systems (immune, endocrine, nervous, respiratory, cardiovascular) work together to promote optimum health. It is well-known that heart rate is related to emotions and that both good and bad emotions trigger changes in heart rate.

Canadian researchers investigated whether gratitude could promote cardiac coherence. Fifty-six adults were randomly assigned to one of two groups: gratitude and memorable events.[77] The gratitude group was asked to consider people, events, or times for which they are particularly grateful and to remember the feelings of gratitude associated with that person, event, or item. This reflection process was completed for five minutes, twice per week, for a total of four weeks. Thoughts and feelings were recorded in a journal. For the memorable event group, participants were asked to recall a memorable event and to re-experience the feelings associated with that event. To collect physiological data, participants were evaluated by electrocardiography and continuous monitoring of blood pressure and heart rate. Baseline measurements were taken prior to random assignment to one of the groups. At the conclusion of the trial, the participants in the gratitude group reported higher life satisfaction and self-esteem and experienced more time in cardiac coherence.

Stage B heart failure (SBHF) involves structural heart disease (systolic left ventricular dysfunction) without any current or prior symptoms of heart failure. Inflammation is a contributing factor to the progression of heart failure and proinflammatory mediators are released even prior to symptoms appearing. A group of researchers hypothesized that gratitude could help improve the quality of life among adults with SBHF.[78] Seventy men and women were randomly assigned to a gratitude intervention or control (standard treatment). Blood was drawn to assess proinflammatory markers and resting heart rate measured prior to, during, and after intervention. The gratitude group maintained a gratitude journal for eight weeks. Participants in both groups completed a gratitude questionnaire at the beginning, middle, and end of the study. What researchers found was that participants in the gratitude group reported greater gratitude, experienced reduced inflammatory biomarkers related to SBHF progression, and increased parasympathetic heart rate variability responses. Altogether, the results suggest that gratitude reduced disease activity and progression to improve quality of life.

Grateful people are more likely to engage in healthy self-care behaviors like eating better, exercise, and getting proactive medical care. A large-scale survey of 962 Swiss adults concluded that grateful individuals experience better physical health, in part because of better psychological health, tendency to engage in healthy activities, and willingness to seek help for health concerns.[79] Remarkably, gratitude seems to replenish willpower to help you stop overeating or overindulging.[80] In other words, by maintaining an attitude of gratitude, you are more likely to take care of yourself, which benefits both your physical and mental/emotional health.

A story is told of how gratitude changed a janitor's life. Being a janitor is a thankless and behind-the-scenes job. It frequently involves dirty jobs that others probably don't like—like cleaning a public restroom. A woman worked as a janitor at the same company for more than twenty years, faithfully keeping the facilities clean and orderly. The company changed ownership, and the new owner wanted to express appreciation to each of the employees. She did so by writing a personal thank-you card and having her assistant hand deliver them to each employee.

When the janitor received her card, she was overcome with emotion and asked if she could be excused from work. She was so touched by the simple gesture of the new owner that she needed the rest of the day to process her emotions. Thinking she was sick, the assistant let her go home. A few days later, the owner received word that this janitor had not ever received as much as a verbal thank-you in her twenty-plus years of dedicated service. Additionally, working a thankless job for over two decades, she had decided the change of ownership was a good time to quit. In fact, she had planned to offer her notice the very day she received her card.

That simple gesture from the new owner changed the janitor's mind. She no longer wanted to quit but, for the first time in her career, felt noticed and appreciated. Are there "janitors" in your life that you are overlooking? Are there dedicated individuals that are going unnoticed and who are underappreciated? If so, seek them out and express gratitude.

Fostering an attitude of gratitude doesn't take a significant amount of effort. It can be as simple as taking a few minutes daily to contemplate on your blessings or documenting them in a gratitude journal.

Acknowledge what you have. Whenever you find yourself envious of another person's things or life, think of three to five things that you have that you are grateful for. There is always something to be grateful for even during difficult times. Besides, you can be sure that another person has it worse than you and is looking at you with the same envy you are looking at another person.

Verbalize gratitude. Saying thank you is a simple but profound gesture. Honor and give thanks for the little things around you and for simple acts people do for you. Say thank you for running hot and cold water, a reliable vehicle to get to and from where you want to go, the beauty of birds chirping, or when a person opens the door for you. You can verbalize gratitude for just about anything.

Intentionally notice things around you. We are each busy and frequently forget to observe the beauty around us. From a beautiful sunset to an animal-shaped cloud, the sound of soft rain to the smell of fresh oranges, and from the quick smile of a passerby to the smell of flowers, appreciate and express gratitude for the simple things. Find the ordinary extraordinary whenever possible.

Model gratitude for others. Just because those around you aren't grateful doesn't mean you shouldn't be. Break the cycle and express gratitude more to individuals who tend not to express it themselves. Express gratitude through words, writing, small gifts, or acts of service. Doing so will help you appreciate the goodness in your own life. Children, especially, respond to your actions more than your words.

Keep a gratitude journal. While thinking of things you are grateful for is helpful, actually writing them down works wonders. A journal provides the opportunity to revisit things you were grateful for in the past when you have days that gratitude is more difficult. Documenting your blessings allows for a deeper examination of what you're grateful for.

Pay it forward. A superb way to foster feelings of gratitude is to pay it forward. Paying it forward spreads kindness to others and is a physical way of saying thanks for kindness we have received. For instance, maybe the person ahead of you in the fast-food drive-through pays for your meal, and you pay it forward by paying for the person behind you. This has often lead to a chain of dozens of people paying it forward.

Gratitude attacks the emotions and traits that keep people divided, such as anger, impulsiveness, and hostility. Additionally, it strengthens our healthy, authentic relationship with others. It may even be the bridge to help us get along with individuals who have differing belief systems. Indeed, gratitude has a healing power that mends hearts and advances unity. Those most adept at gratitude have an awareness that finds the positive side of any situation. No matter your situation, find something to be grateful for and then let that gratitude grow within your heart until you discover the exceptional curative power of gratitude in your life.

> The heart that gives thanks is a happy one, for we cannot feel thankful and unhappy at the same time.
>
> —Douglas Wood

CHAPTER 4

POSITIVITY

Attitude is a little thing that makes a big difference.

—Winston Churchill

We can't always control what comes our way in life, but we can control our attitudes in response to those things that do. Fostering a positive attitude—a state of mind where you expect good things to happen—will help you cope more easily with daily life. A positive attitude increases happiness, contentment, resilience, and success. There is a strong association between positivity and enhanced relationships, health, and accomplishment.

A positive attitude begins with positive thinking. Think of your mind as a magnet: you attract what you spend the most time thinking about. Our inner voices, or self-talk, combine conscious thoughts with subconscious feelings, beliefs, and biases to interpret and process daily experiences. Self-talk can be both negative and positive. Unfortunately, humans are predisposed to self-defeating talk. That voice in your head that says you aren't smart enough to speak in front of your neighbors at the school board meeting. The voice that says you aren't pretty enough. That voice that says you're a failure as a father and provider. That voice that says you are doomed to experience defeat. That voice that says your past mistakes are too injurious to overcome. It's said that hindsight is 20-20 because we see the results of past decisions. It is not beneficial to judge your past mistakes based on what you know today. Every single person regrets a past decision and wishes he or she could change it somehow. Give your past self a break and understand you did your best with the knowledge you had at the time. Since most of our self-talk is negative, we need to reframe as much of it as possible to promote positivity.

Developing daily habits can help you maintain positivity:

Smile. For such a simple gesture, smiles are astonishingly powerful. Smiles are contagious. Just look at an infant's smile and it is hard not to return the gesture. Indeed, smiles are so powerful that when subjects in a study were shown pictures of smiling people and asked to frown, their facial expressions involuntarily imitated the smile instead.[81] This may be because the part of the brain responsible for the facial expression of smiling resides in the cingulate cortex, an unconscious, automatic response area of the brain.[82] So, smiling at someone benefits both you and them if they respond in kind.

Surveys suggest women smile more than men on average, especially when they believe they are being observed.[83] This may be because women tend to use smiling as a way to diffuse tension in situations. Other theories suggest that men and women are conditioned to express emotions, such as smiling, differently. In any case, a genuine smile increases perceived social attractiveness, kindness, and intelligence.

Smiling is far from an involuntary response to a positive situation or experience. When you smile, signals from your brain travel to muscles responsible for smiling (zygomaticus major—controls the corners of your mouth; and orbicularis oculi—muscles that surround your eye socket and reveal a genuine smile), and that distinct symbol of joyfulness appears on your face. But that doesn't end the smiling response. Contraction of smiling muscles initiates a positive feedback loop that sends a response signal to the brain that reinforces feelings of joy. Joyful feelings cause you to smile more, and the loop of smiling and joy continues.

Smiling can change your brain through this powerful feedback loop. The signals sent from the face to the brain strengthen positive emotions that cause the brain to release neuropeptides associated with happiness and activate feel-good neurotransmitters like dopamine, serotonin, and endorphins.[84] At the same time, smiling reduces psychophysiological stress by regulating stress hormones.[85] Smile often. Doing so creates a symbiotic relationship that allows you and those who return the smile to release chemicals in the brain that improve your lives.

Consume positive media. You are what you eat is a literal expression that represents the fact that what you eat or drink is broken down and becomes part of your cells and tissues. The same is true for what our mind consumes in the form of media (books, movies, social media, music, etc.). The mind is nurtured by how much positive media we make available to it as "nutrients."

For a long time, researchers focused almost exclusively on the harmful effects of media and found plenty to be wary of.[86,87,88,89] More recently, researchers have also identified positive benefits of media as long as the media itself is positive in nature. Uplifting and inspiring media can help us become more prosocial—a state where we want to improve and help others.[90] Specifically, consuming media that portrays moral virtues (e.g., gratitude, loyalty, generosity, justice) elicits specific emotional responses that motivate us to embody those moral virtues. So, you become what your mind consumes.

Research also suggests that media can influence how we view the world. Negative media reinforces that the world is a dangerous place and full of mean people. On the flip side, inspiring and positive media shifts our world perception toward goodness, kindness, and safety, and increases compassion and love toward humanity.[91,92] Excess consumption of meaningless and negative media has created a cynical view of people and the world. Limiting our exposure to it can tilt the global paradigm to one of compassion and love. You get to choose what media you consume, and your choices can dramatically affect your health, happiness, and view of others and the world. Wouldn't it be better to choose uplifting, inspiring, and positive media as much as possible?

Focus on the good (in you, your life, and life's situations). No individual escapes adversity, challenges, and difficulty in life. These are universal human experiences. Once we accept this, we can move forward and focus on the good in our lives. What consumes your mind, controls your life. Despite life's challenges, we can choose to fill our minds with good thoughts and remember our blessings. Two opposing thoughts cannot exist in our minds simultaneously, so there's a constant battle between good and negative thoughts for space in our mind. Put your support behind the good thoughts by seeing the good inside of you, in your life, and in life's experiences. Visualize good things in your life. When you focus on the good, good is amplified.

- Start with good health habits: healthy eating, daily physical activity, hydration, adequate sleep, and so on.
- Repeat positive phrases out loud every day. For example, "I have a wonderful family" or "I am beautiful."
- Ask yourself if this frustrating situation will matter in an hour, tomorrow, week, or month? If not, don't let it occupy your mind.
- Express gratitude daily because it forces you to find good things you are thankful for.
- Train your mind to search for the good in each person and situation.
- As Mahatma Gandhi said, "Be the good you wish to see in the world." Can't find something good to focus on? Be that good yourself.
- Challenge negative thoughts and ask if this is a big-T "Truth" or a little-t "truth." In other words, is this my perception of the truth, or is it the actual truth? A quick example is you going to a work party where no one talks

70

to you. You think it's because no one likes you (truth), but perhaps the others are just as nervous or focused on deadlines as you are and don't feel like talking (Truth).

- Surround yourself with people who do good.
- Unplug from media more often. It is very beneficial to spend less time endlessly scrolling.

Avoid feelings of entitlement. You aren't owed anything, so replace feelings of entitlement with an understanding that you need to work hard for what you want. Entitlement is a negative personality trait justified by feelings of envy, jealousy, anger, and frustration. People who feel entitled believe that they inherently deserve privileges, material things, or recognition for things they did not earn. Thomas Sowell was right when he said, "What exactly is your 'fair share' of what 'someone else' has worked for?" Far from stating that a person should never receive help or assistance, this just means that it should be willingly given and not coerced or demanded. People with compassion will freely give to those in need, but they are not duty bound to give indefinitely to people who expect a free ride. Entitlement goes hand in hand with pessimism and is the antithesis of self-help and optimism.

Entitlement is the epitome of the me-first and my-needs-supersede-the-needs-of-others attitude, where people falsely believe the world should revolve around a single person—them! People with a sense of entitlement—often called an entitlement complex—usually display it in the following ways:

- exaggerated sense of self-importance
- impose unrealistic demands on family, friends, employers, colleagues, and society in general
- seek attention in aggressive ways
- lack empathy and an inability to recognize the needs and wants of others
- unwillingness to compromise
- exercise self-pity

- lack of ability to recognize others as equals
- embellishment of one's own achievements and dismissal of other's achievements
- manipulate others and punish them passively (e.g., silent treatment, gossip) when they don't get what they want
- view others as competitive threats
- regard the rules that apply to others as not applicable to themselves

Entitlement is dangerous because it is self-serving and gets people nowhere in life. Eventually, it leads to an attitude of hopelessness and a general view that the world is a nasty place. Why? Because entitled individuals have yielded control of their own life and destiny to others. If you recognize entitlement tendencies in your life, find the motivation to change. Doing so will give you greater control of your life and success, freeing you from reliance on others.

Limit complaining. Complaining, or whining, is a toxic emotion that quickly spoils your emotional environment. The fact is nobody likes to hear it, and it's harmful to your health. Just a half-hour of daily complaining, both complaining and being complained to, damages your brain.[93] Specifically, complaining shrinks your hippocampus—an area of the brain critical to memory, intelligence, emotions, and problem-solving. Ineffective complaining damages your mental health. As an unhealthy coping mechanism, it increases both depression and anxiety. Complaining also floods the bloodstream with the stress hormone cortisol. Chronically elevated cortisol levels can contribute to a variety of health problems, such as depression, poor sleep, high blood pressure, heart disease, lowered immune function, weight gain, and digestive disturbances.

Occasionally, complaining is necessary, but if you must complain, you should do so in a reasonable manner. Complaints should begin with a positive statement rather than an angry outburst. For example, if you purchased a pizza from your favorite pizza parlor and they skimped on toppings, start by expressing your loyalty to the restaurant and how you normally get great pizza before expressing dissatisfaction. Have a purpose for your complaint. If you're just grumbling to grumble, don't do it. Instead, identify what you want to achieve first. Back to the pizza discussion, maybe a replacement pizza. Maintain your calm and complain in a kind way. Consider who you are complaining to. The counter person probably didn't make your pizza and, in all likelihood, doesn't own the restaurant, nor does she make the company policies. Berating her will not help your issue. Express your concern as truthfully and nicely as possible. End with a positive statement. "I'd love to keep coming back here for more pizza." Whatever the outcome, let the situation go and don't let it ruin your day. Dwelling on a minor irritation can be detrimental to your mental and physical health.

Express gratitude. This was covered extensively in the previous chapter, but it bears repeating. Gratitude is an antidote to adverse situations and fosters optimism. Increased optimism means more hope, which is the emotional framework that reinforces happiness.

Surround yourself with positive people. Positive people build you up and invite traits that highlight your full potential. We are heavily influenced by our environment and act as sponges when it comes to mannerisms, speech, and activities. Based on this, it stands to reason that the people you spend the most time with will have a greater impact on your personality. You will absorb fragments of their character, and they will start to act more like you, without even knowing it. Negative people drain your energy, while positive people foster a nurturing environment that encourages you to be better.

You can't always choose who you are around—for example, coworkers—but whenever possible surround yourself with positive people. Reflect on how people make you feel and spend more time among people who uplift you and whose presence makes you happy. You may need to make changes in your social life by eliminating people who zap your strength and bring you down. But in the end, this removes negativity in your life and clears space for people who will renew your energy.

Turn challenges into opportunities. The challenging moments of life always offer a learning experience, but they may also present great growth opportunities. Although difficult during adversity, training yourself to look for opportunities during challenges produces a powerful mindset shift. Successfully facing challenges allows you to come out stronger in the end.

Successful individuals have obtained a distinctive mentality that permits them to attack challenges differently. Rather than focusing on the burdens involved, they see opportunities to learn, adjust, improve, and develop in ways that make them better off than before the problem presented itself. This view detaches them from the stress of the problem and allows them greater focus on responses to the problem. While we all probably wish we could flip a switch for our brains to adopt this mindset, it takes time and effort to retrain your brain.

First, adopt a problem-solving mindset. Problems occur each day, both large and small, that need to be solved. Second, you need to change your perspective. Irrational emotions interfere with seeing things as they truly are as opposed to how we may falsely perceive them to be. Disconnect from the emotions of the obstacle and reorient your thoughts to identify the correct reality of the problem. Problems should not be perceived as insurmountable but merely detours on the way to your final destination. You wouldn't cancel an amazing family trip and go home because of a roadblock. You'd find another way to get where you want to go. Next, learn from your mistakes. Not every solution will work as intended, and successful individuals absorb information and details from failing moments. Fourth, focus on what can be done.

Don't waste time and effort on factors outside your control. Lastly, maintain a positive attitude while attacking the problem. An unshakable belief in your abilities can go a long way in overcoming obstacles. Commitment to your goals, the right mindset, a well-thought-out plan, creative solutions, and emphasis on what you can do, propel you to success.

Practice mindfulness. During the last several years, mindfulness has become a major topic of pop culture. It is no longer something from the fringes that only hippies practice. Mindfulness involves maintaining awareness of and accepting your thoughts, feelings, bodily sensations, and surrounding environment without judgment. Practicing it permits careful observance of what occupies your mind and life. Optimism requires mindful monitoring of our thoughts and the purposeful addition of positive thoughts into our day.

Mindfulness improves your overall well-being. It balances your mood, reduces stress, depression, and anxiety, improves emotional resilience, preserves cognitive abilities, and generally brings happiness and optimism into your life.[94,95,96,97,98] In addition to the mental and emotional benefits of mindfulness, it also relieves pain, enhances immune system activity, reduces the risk of heart disease, and helps you cope with chronic and potentially life-threatening disorders.[99,100,101,102] Researchers are only beginning to discover the many benefits of practicing regular mindfulness.

Shun a victim mentality. In this section, we are not discussing people who are the victims of unlawful, criminal, or unethical acts of others. We are talking about those who wish to portray themselves as victims for personal gain. A victim mentality is a condition of alleging harm or suffering in efforts to get people to feel sorry for you and to use as an excuse for personal benefit. These individuals deceptively weaponize being a victim to gain advantage over others.

To extract resources from others, self-absorbed individuals make public spectacles out of real, fabricated, or perceived suffering, categorize themselves as victims, and demand reparation for their pain. Studies show that people with maladaptive personality traits known as the "Dark Triad"—narcissism, psychopathy, and Machiavellianism (a personality trait characterized by manipulation, callousness, and indifference to morality)—are most likely to engage in a victim mentality.[103] These individuals have a greater sensitivity to insults, are more easily offended, and are less tolerant of disagreement. They are disproportionately watchful for offenses and seek to draw as much attention as possible to the alleged offense when identified. Even the rich practice a victim mentality. They do so to remove any obligation to contribute to society. When wealthy individuals garner sympathy from the public, the public expects less from the wealthy. This was on full display when Meghan Markle and Prince Harry complained to Oprah Winfrey alleging racism and lack of support for mental health issues from Prince Harry's royal family. Whether the allegations are true or not misses the point, we have a multimillionaire couple complaining to a multibillionaire talk show host about how oppressed they are and how terrible their lives are. For people with victim mentalities, feelings of pessimism, self-pity, and misery are common and constant. In reality, no person, institution, or organization oppresses a person more than his or her own mind when that person assumes a victim mentality.

Obviously, a victim mentality is not compatible with positivity. A perceived lack of control over one's personal success and failure leaves practicers of a victim mentality feeling helpless, angry, and without blame for what occurs in their lives. If you believe you are simply a victim of your circumstances, nothing is ever your fault, or the world has treated you unfairly, it's time to take personal responsibility and own your own happiness. One challenge will be that many who reverse their victim mentalities feel an emptiness within because they are no longer victims.

The first step in conquering a victim mentality is developing a willingness to forgo the benefits it provides: financial gain, attention, validation, and lack of responsibility and blame. Second, recognize a need for greater personal responsibility and accept accountability for your life. Create a list of areas of your life you would like to improve and manage more effectively. Third, acknowledge negative feelings toward people, organizations, or things, then seek to forgive and move forward. You don't need to stay in a harmful relationship, but grudges only hurt the person holding them. Fourth, express gratitude for your blessings. You have much to be grateful for and can always find someone else in the world who has it worse. Think of these individuals whenever you are tempted to adopt a woe-is-me attitude. Fifth, keep in mind that you aren't perfect, and you will occasionally slip back into your victim mentality. That's OK. Be nice to yourself anyway. Lastly, consider turning your focus outward and helping others. Adding value to others through service, large or small, shifts your focus away from your own problems.

Epitomizing the American dream of rags to riches through hard work and dedication, Shahid Khan is a Pakistani-born naturalized American entrepreneur. Born in Lahore, Pakistan, in 1950, Khan emigrated to the United States at age sixteen with only $500 to his name. He took a job as a dishwasher while attending the University of Illinois's Engineering School. Despite having very little money, he maintained a positive attitude that he could achieve success if he worked hard.

After graduation, he accepted a job at a company called Flex-N-Gate, which manufactured aftermarket automotive parts. Khan oversaw the inefficient process of welding together multiple parts to create an automotive bumper for seven years. Noting the lack of innovation in the industry, he left Flex-N-Gate and formed his own company, Bumper Works, to design a revolutionary one-piece bumper sold directly to big auto manufacturers.

Fortunately, he convinced General Motors to buy his new bumper for their imported Isuzu pickup called the Chevrolet Luv. His celebrated success was short-lived, however, because Flex-N-Gate sued him for stealing trade secrets and violating his fiduciary responsibilities. Armed with the cheapest lawyer he could hire and his own personal study of the law, he eventually won the lawsuit and acquired Flex-N-Gate for only their meager book value assets in 1980.

Another hurdle came when General Motors required that his company increase production from two hundred bumpers per day to forty thousand. Failure to ramp up production would mean General Motors could leverage a clause in his contract to use his designs without him. He formed a positive relationship with Isuzu, followed by Mazda and Toyota, that saved his business. By 2011, more than two-thirds of automobiles sold in the United States used Flex-N-Gate's innovative bumper.

As of March 2021, his net worth is estimated at $8 billion. Khan could easily have given up when he was sued or when General Motors threatened to execute an unfavorable clause in his contract, but he didn't. His positive can-do attitude has not only made him successful in the auto parts business, but he now owns the NFL's Jacksonville Jaguars, All Elite Wrestling, and is a major financier of Black News Channel, a twenty-four-hour cable news channel targeting the African American demographic.

Just like gratitude has many benefits, a positive attitude benefits your well-being in many ways. A positive attitude keeps your focus on positive outcomes and favorable results.

Most people want healthy relationships and a pleasant social life. Anyone who has been in a relationship of any kind knows that they are not always on good terms. Establishing an attitude of optimism can create more resilience to weather the hard times when people within a relationship have a disagreement. Research found that positive individuals better respond to negative moments in relationships and as a result are more able to cultivate healthy and appropriate responses to disagreements.[104] What this research suggests is that positive people make better friends, colleagues, neighbors, family, and partners.

Knowing that negative emotions like depression and anxiety lead to poor outcomes in people with heart disease, researchers reviewed how positive psychological constructs (the major construct in the research was optimism) affected people with heart disease.[105] Exploration of the eleven included studies found that positive constructs were associated with reduced rates of rehospitalization and death. Other research concluded that positive psychological well-being contributes to the prevention of cardiovascular disorders.[106] Perhaps practicing positivity should be prescribed alongside traditional treatments for heart disease.

Positivity can make you a more productive worker than your peers. Who knows, maybe your positive attitude will be the difference for your next promotion? Evaluating the workplace benefits of positivity in two separate industries—financial services and health care—researchers discovered that positivity improves work performance.[107] Those displaying positive traits increased their self-confidence over time, leading to increased success when compared to negative individuals that focused on their mistakes and therefore were more likely to fail again. Employers who create positive atmospheres consistently have staff that are higher performers.

In a somewhat literal way, optimism wills positive results into your life. Your focus on positivity triggers the release of biochemicals that positively modify your health and mood. Your cells respond to these biochemicals by adapting their structures and functions, and since your cells make up your tissues and organs, you experience improved health. A positive attitude takes practice, but it is well worth it. Ultimately, optimism helps you defeat false thinking that your life is not under your control and nothing you can do will break free of control by the ruling elite.

> Nothing can stop the man with the right mental attitude from achieving his goal; nothing on earth can help the man with the wrong mental attitude.
>
> —Thomas Jefferson

CHAPTER 5

SERVICE AND CHARITY

No one is useless in this world who lightens
the burden of it to anyone else.

—Charles Dickens

Service is a transformative action for the purpose of helping
another person. Its transformative potential lies in the fact that it
has the potential to improve the lives of both the person receiving
and performing the service. Service means putting the interests of
others above your own. It is giving without expecting anything in
return. It elevates the receiver and is a source of joy and fulfillment
for the performer. Imagine a world where people spent more time
serving one another—wouldn't the world be a more beautiful and
better place?

Charity—the willful and unconditional extension of kindness and
love to others—is the impetus to serve. We can learn a lot from
Mark Twain's statement that "kindness is the language which the
deaf can hear and the blind can see." Charity improves human
relationships because it brings meaning and richness to our lives.
We connect with others and nurture feelings of love and
compassion when we help others.

The Christmas Orange is a tender story about those who have very
little giving to someone in need. A nine-year-old boy named Jake
lived in an orphanage all his life. Throughout the year, the ten
children in the orphanage subsisted on meager donations from the

local townspeople, but at Christmas, there was a cherished Christmas orange. Christmas was the only time such a delicious treat was provided to each child. Unfortunately for Jake, he managed to track a small amount of mud from his shoes onto new carpet in the orphanage. The punishment—no Christmas orange—was devastating to a boy who had so little. He cried and spent Christmas Day alone, mourning the loss of his precious orange. After kneeling to pour his soul out to God in prayer, he felt a gentle tap on his shoulder. Quickly, an object was placed in his hands, and the giver disappeared into the darkness. Struggling to clearly see the object in the darkness, he finally made out what appeared to be an orange. But not an ordinary orange. Inside, a patchwork orange peel were orange wedges from nine separate oranges graciously donated to him by each of the nine other orphans. Sharing what we most value, even if we get less, is the true spirit of charity.

Said Brigham Young, "But how are we to be made happy? There is one course—love the Giver more than the gift." We have been told forever that money can't buy happiness, but this is only partly true. What makes the difference is who you spend the money on. Surveying a group of Americans about their income and what they spend their money on, researchers found that, regardless of income level, people who spent money on others were significantly happier than those who spent money on themselves.[108] Anne Frank added to this conversation by stating, "No one has ever become poor by giving." People don't become poor by giving because they are rewarded exponentially and far beyond material wealth by doing so.

In another sense, charity includes a willingness to forgive someone who has hurt us. It is not taking advantage of another's weakness. Charity shines when we don't judge, criticize, or categorize others. Charity is accepting the differences and weaknesses of others. Charity is expecting the best out of each person we encounter.

Genuine charity is the selfless gift of unconditional love. True charity inspires service to others because you can't bear seeing others without. It makes life more meaningful for others even when we are called to serve at inconvenient times.

Opportunities for service are abundant in our personal, professional, and civic life. One need not know the person they give service to either. Random acts of kindness and compassion can make a big difference. Contrary to popular belief, service doesn't have to involve money or major acts. Simple acts such as listening, a hug, a smile, visiting the sick and lonely, taking in a neighbor's trash can, opening the door for someone, and much more are still service and can be very meaningful to the receiver. Often, small acts of service are all that is necessary to lift and bless another.

Helping others face their own challenges changes your perspective on your own. Often, it helps you be more grateful for what you have, especially if your challenges seem smaller by comparison. We often take basic necessities for granted, such as clean, running water, shelter, and food, until we spend time with others living without these necessities. Henry B. Eyring said, "We must notice the tribulation of others and try to help. That will be especially hard when we are being sorely tested ourselves. But we will discover as we lift another's burden, even a little, that our backs are strengthened and we sense a light in the darkness." Service is uplifting and can cultivate gratitude as we consider people who are living in profoundly difficult situations.

Service boosts self-esteem. Genuine acts of kindness that improve other's lives allow us opportunities to see the impacts of our service. We see that we are adding value to another person. In a direct way, you also recognize you are valued. You understand your important purpose in the lives of others.

In 2007, Thomas S. Monson related the following story of selfless service that involved putting the needs of others over one's own.[109] "I learned recently of loving service given to a mother when her children were very young. Frequently she would be up in the middle of the night tending to the needs of her little ones, as mothers do. Often her friend and neighbor across the street would come over the next day and say, 'I saw your lights on in the middle of the night and know you were up with the children. I'm going to take them to my house for a couple of hours while you take a nap.' Said this grateful mother, 'I was so thankful for her welcome offer, it wasn't until this had happened many times that I realized if she had seen my lights on in the middle of the night, she was up with one of her children as well and needed a nap just as much as I did. She taught me a great lesson, and I've since tried to be as observant as she was in looking for opportunities to serve others.'" A selfless act of service changed the mindset of the person receiving the service so that she was more motivated to look for others to serve.

This brings us to the concept of paying it forward (an expression describing the beneficiary of a good deed perpetuating the kindness they received by giving to others instead of the original person who served them). In the story above, the grateful mother received an act of service, and it prompted within her a desire to serve others. Kindness begets kindness. Service perpetuates service. By serving others, you can spark a chain of reactions that leads to multiple other people being served.

Research suggests that opportunities to serve others result in a stronger sense of purpose and meaning in life, which leads to improved well-being.[110] Indeed, service can be the difference between happiness and meaninglessness in life. While satisfying your own needs and wants brings happiness, serving others brings more meaningfulness to life.

It comes as no surprise that studies show serving others can improve your mental and emotional health. Researchers call this a "helper's high." Similar to a runner's high, volunteering, charitable donations, and even just thinking about donating money to a good cause can release feel-good chemicals that activate the pleasure center of the brain.[111] In addition, people engaged in service tend to have lower levels of the stress hormone cortisol. The science of service and volunteering is revealing what those of us who have occupied our time in service have known for decades—serving others brings joy into your own life.

Helping others also improves your physical health and lifespan. One study found that older individuals who volunteered for at least two hundred hours per year (roughly four hours per week) decreased their risk of high blood pressure by 40 percent.[112] Only the amount of time spent volunteering, not the type of volunteer activity, changed the benefits according to the study. This suggests that you can volunteer to do just about anything and reduce your risk of high blood pressure—something affecting nearly 75 percent of older adults over age sixty.[113] Researchers have also documented that volunteering can increase your lifespan. Want more time with your grandchildren or to travel? You may want to consider helping others. Data from nearly thirteen thousand adults over fifty years of age showed that those who volunteered for about two hours per week had a reduced risk of mortality and fewer functional limitations than older adults who don't volunteer.[114] The good thing is the data showed these were quality years with higher physical activity and improved mental and emotional health.

Interestingly, evidence demonstrates that people struggling with their own challenges are more motivated to overcome adversity when they give advice rather than receive it. A series of studies including more than 2,200 people found that when middle school students mentored younger students about studying, they spent more time focused on their own homework.[115] Overweight people were more motivated to lose weight themselves when they taught others weight-loss strategies. People struggling to save money were driven to be more financially responsible after giving financial advice. Individuals seeking jobs who taught others job-seeking skills were inspired by their own advice. And people who had tempers felt more encouraged to control their anger when they gave advice to others on the subject. It appears that giving advice instills confidence and ambition in the person giving it, particularly when helping someone through a challenge we ourselves are facing.

Few things build stronger bonds than service. It forges bonds between people serving together and bonds among givers and receivers of service. Service engages you with other individuals and your community, creating a deeper feeling of connection. Service improves relationships because we temporarily take our focus off ourselves and focus on others. Service may even improve strained relationships. Frequently, conflict in relationships (among family, friendships, work, neighbors, etc.) has to do with ego. We are selfish and intent on serving our own wants. Service provides the opportunity to focus on others, momentarily removing our egos from the relationship. Regularly practicing service makes it a habit and changes our attitudes. When our attitudes improve, so do our relationships.

Serving also helps us bridge divides between us and others. It is easy to serve those we love and care about, and not too difficult to help strangers. However, most people find it challenging to serve people we dislike or disagree with. Despite this, we must understand that we grow to love those we serve. Abraham Lincoln said, "I don't like that man. I must get to know him better." We may have hastily judged the person we dislike, and getting to know them could turn this dislike into understanding and eventually a positive relationship. What better way to get to know a person than to serve them? Any act of service opens our heart to love the person we are serving.

You may find it hard to believe, but a professional musician named Daryl Davis spent thirty years befriending members of the Ku Klux Klan (KKK), despite being a man of color. Why did he do this? He wanted to understand the reason behind the KKK's entrenched racism and end it not by vehemently opposing it but through two-way communication. He encountered violent racism while attending a scout parade at the age of ten. A group of white people shouted racial slurs and threw bottles just because of the color of his skin. He could have reacted negatively and developed a hatred for white people because of this, but instead, he wanted to answer his burning question "How can you hate me when you don't know me?"

He was unable to find his answers in books, so as an adult, he asked members of the KKK directly. Through his investigations, he befriended the Grand Dragon of the KKK in Maryland, Roger Kelly. They became close friends despite their major ideological differences. Kelly even invited Davis to be his daughter's godfather. Eventually, Kelly left the KKK and gifted his KKK robe to Davis. Over thirty years, Davis has convinced two hundred Klan members of their errant ways and talked them into leaving the racist organization. He now keeps a collection of Klan robes as trophies and proof racism can be defeated. Davis represents how compassion and understanding can enact significant change and build bonds among people with opposing values. His tactics show that speaking truth, after understanding the other person, is mightier than legal efforts or violence in changing others. If Davis can strip individuals of hateful ignorance and violent tendencies, we can certainly mend differences among neighbors, coworkers, family, and friends.

Service truly is transformative. It changes people's lives for the better, and each individual it touches belongs to a community, which is also improved. The world would be an entirely different place if each of us made time for service each week.

> He who lives only unto himself withers and dies, while he who forgets himself in the service of others grows and blossoms in this life and in eternity.

> —Gordon B. Hinckley

CHAPTER 6

LOVE

> Love is always bestowed as a gift—freely, willingly, and without expectation. We don't love to be loved; we love to love.
>
> —Leo Buscaglia

Genuine love is more than an expression of words; it requires action and involves sacrifice. All too often, love is merely associated with romance and relationships. However, to truly love someone is deeper and more powerful than romantic attraction. Unless fortified by genuine love, romantic love is fleeting, jealous, and possessive. Much like service, love encompasses unselfishly putting the needs of others before our own. Being loved is as necessary as blood and oxygen. Humans have a need to feel loved, valued, and appreciated. Few things will accomplish this more than seeing them not as they are now but as they may become and treating them accordingly.

Unfortunately, many believe the myth that an angelic being (Cupid) is responsible for love or that it just happens involuntarily. Others suppose, as popular culture teaches, that we must simply wait for a "prince" or "princess" to be inserted into our lives so we can be swept off our feet and live happily ever after. Again, this involves a narrow view of love as only related to romance. As a consequence, many people passively wait to be shot by an arrow or be acted upon by love freely floating in the air or delivered in the form of an illusory love interest. What these people fail to understand is that love requires action.

Love is the core of the two greatest commandments defined by Christ in the Bible. When asked which was the greatest commandment in the law, He responded emphatically, "Thou shalt love the Lord thy God with all thy heart, and with all thy soul, and with all thy mind. . . [and] thou shalt love thy neighbor as thyself."[116] Who is our neighbor? The reality is that it is all of humanity without limitation. We get to choose our friends, but our neighbors are chosen for us. We are humans first and foremost. Division by qualities—gender, ethnicity, nationality, political ideologies—seeks to deprive us of that connection. The second question then becomes how do we love our neighbor. By following the platinum rule to treat others as they want to be treated.

A woman who loves her neighbor will not only avoid causing her neighbor harm but will actively seek to help her. Neighborly love does not abuse people as purely instrumental for our own selfish goals but treats them in their own best interests. Some of the greatest opportunities to demonstrate authentic love will occur within the walls of our own homes and among our families. Among the most challenging types of love is love toward those we dislike. This type of love takes desire, self-discipline, patience, humility, and a great deal of practice. Love must be practiced in each of our relationships: family, friendships, business, dating and marriage, school, work, and all other interactions with our fellow man.

One of the greatest examples of love is the love that exudes from mothers. Talk about sacrifice! Mothers frequently and selflessly redirect their entire lives for their children. Goals are shifted, habits changed, and objectives take on new meaning as they tirelessly seek the good of their treasured child. Loving mothers consistently put their children's needs and wants above their own.

A child's love is reciprocated as evidenced by the most common question asked of a father, "Where's Mom?"

With so much hate in the world, the major antidote must be love. Two things in opposition cannot occupy the same space simultaneously—light and darkness, water and emptiness, love and hate. Nelson Mandela said, "If people can learn to hate, they can be taught to love, for love comes more naturally to the human heart than its opposite." Shakespeare taught us this in *Romeo and Juliet*. Despite hatred and the feuding between their families— the Capulets and Montagues, Romeo and Juliet's love for one another overpowers learned hate. In his dramatic play, Shakespeare showed that love is a more powerful force than hate. And he was right!

Sometimes, we stake our identity and self-worth based on our groups. Our limited emotional resources are then predominantly given to this group at the expense of any person outside the group. Individuals who rise above this group-first mentality have a more meaningful impact on the lives of those they encounter. Their broader view of who their neighbor is and connection to humanity drives their love outward to influence a wider audience.

Amid the horrors and tragedies of the Holocaust that took the lives of more than ten million people, mostly Jews, brave people risked their lives because of their love for humanity. Hungarian businessman-turned-diplomat Raoul Wallenberg is credited for saving thousands—perhaps as many as a hundred thousand— Hungarian Jews by providing authentic-looking documents and setting up safe houses. Dutch educator Johan van Hulst smuggled Jewish children out of Amsterdam during the Nazi occupation of the Netherlands. A member of the Polish Underground and a Catholic social worker, Irena Sendler helped save 2,500 Jewish children from the Warsaw Ghetto by providing them false documents and shelter. She continued her heroic work even after being captured and tortured. Georg Ferdinand Duckwitz was a

German member of the Nazi Party assigned as a special envoy to Nazi-occupied Denmark. He risked his career and life by convincing the prime minister of Sweden to allow Danish Jewish refugees to escape to Sweden when he learned they were next to be deported to concentration camps. These are just a few of the many people who saved lives during World War II. Each of these individuals demonstrated a love for humanity (including complete strangers) that was stronger than their fear of harm and death that came to many who defied the Nazis.

You may or may not be surprised that love also provides health benefits, at least for those living in loving relationships. A review of multiple studies found that people in loving marriages required fewer visits to the doctor.[117] Whether this is from your spouse encouraging you to engage in preventive health care or a symptom of love itself, researchers don't know, but it appears loving relationships can maintain your health. Moreover, the same report found that getting married and staying married reduces depression, heavy drinking, and drug abuse in men and women. Other research associated loving relationships with less stress and anxiety, fewer colds, lower blood pressure, better control of pain, faster wound healing, and living longer, happier lives.[118,119,120,121,122,123] Men and women are not meant to be alone, and meaningful relationships filled with reciprocal love make life healthier and happier.

It is much easier to show love to another person when we see them as a human being with a family, goals, and desires. Before we engage in disparaging or ridiculing another person, try to remember that he or she is a son or daughter, perhaps a mother or father or sibling. He or she is affected by a unique set of challenges and experiences that has shaped that person's attitude, personality, beliefs, and so forth. Seek to see others' humanity. Care about what they are going through. Focus on their potential no matter how far they may have sunk. We are all created equal, so treat everyone as equals. Pursue the purity of loving everyone as if they are your brother or sister. Maintain an open mind. Loving others is one of the hardest things to master, but you can do it if you desire to and practice it daily.

> Darkness cannot drive out darkness; only light can do that. Hate cannot drive out hate; only love can do that.
>
> —Dr. Martin Luther King Jr.

CHAPTER 7

COMPASSION AND EMPATHY

> Empathy is about standing in someone else's shoes, feeling with his or her heart, seeing with his or her eyes. Not only is empathy hard to outsource and automate, but it makes the world a better place.
>
> —Daniel H. Pink

Compassion and empathy are similar but distinct. Compassion involves a cognitive understanding of another person's suffering along with a desire to relieve it. Empathy, on the other hand, involves not just the recognition of the situation but a deep understanding of what someone else is feeling and the ability to share the feelings of others. Living a life of empathy and compassion for others, combined with doing the morally right thing, prompts the downfall of the ruling class.

Called self-compassion, true compassion begins with caring for yourself. We should be kind and understanding toward ourselves when we fail, experience disappointment, feel inadequate, or suffer—something very difficult to do for many of us. We are all imperfect beings, and each of us makes mistakes, lots of them, in fact. Instead of mercilessly criticizing yourself, endeavor to respond to yourself the way you would another person in the same situation. If your teammate missed the game-winning goal, would you berate him or her for the next several hours, or would you pat that person on the back and offer words of encouragement? Too commonly, we take the first approach with ourselves and cruelly self-judge and self-criticize. Likewise, don't ignore personal suffering. Acknowledge your feelings and pain—emotional, mental, physical, or spiritual—and do your best to comfort and care for yourself in the moment. Some experts suggest comforting yourself with a physical gesture, such as placing your hand over your heart, wringing your hands, or rubbing the back of your arms. Physical touch gets you out of your head and brings awareness to the physical sensation instead. Another option is to maintain a set of compassionate phrases (see the box below for examples). Seek the help of a trusted loved one, friend, counselor, therapist, or ecclesiastical leader if needed. If you find it difficult to love yourself, it will often be difficult to love others as well.

Compassionate Phrases:

- I am doing the best I can under these challenging circumstances.
- This is a really hard day. Adversity is part of life, and I accept my frustration.
- I'm struggling today like many other people, and like other people, I deserve kindness too.
- I made a mistake, and I can make it right.
- I forgive myself for _____.

Self-compassion is important for healthy relationships because how you treat yourself frequently spills over into how you let others treat you. By being cruel to yourself, you establish a standard for how much abuse you accept from others. Consequently, you end up in abusive and disrespectful relationships. At the same time, if we expect perfection of ourselves, chances are we will transfer those feelings to others we have relationships with. This means you are less likely to give them a break when they make mistakes. Practicing self-compassion means less reliance on the validation of others to recognize your personal value and worth.

Compassion may be more effective than empathy, according to some research. Two neuroscientists conducted experiments comparing empathy and compassion.[124] What they observed was that the brain reacts differently when practicing compassion versus empathy. Empathy activated an area of the brain associated with self-awareness, consciousness, and emotions (the insular cortex) as well as areas of the brain that process pain. On the contrary, compassion activated areas of the brain associated with learning and reward in the decision-making process (the medial orbitofrontal cortex and ventral striatum). Additionally, the empathy group found empathy troublesome and unpleasant, whereas the compassion group felt kinder and more willing to help others. Accordingly, feeling empathy or compassion leads to two different emotional responses that could lead to very different actions. It seems that walking in another person's shoes, although figurative, is as uncomfortable as it sounds in real life if the shoes are too large or too small.

Another study found that humans naturally are self-centered when in a state of comfort, but a part of the brain (the right supramarginal gyrus) recognizes that we are lacking empathy and makes corrections.[125] This part of the brain interprets tactile sensations, perceives body location relative to our environment, and identifies postures and gestures of other people. It is responsible for both empathy and compassion. When this part of the brain is not functioning well, or we need to make very quick decisions, our ability to empathize is very limited. When it functions properly, we are able to perceive the emotional level of others and dissociate our own emotional states from theirs to avoid projecting our feelings on that person.

Some also fear that feeling the pain of others may trigger negative emotions within one's self. Importantly, empathy avoids the confusion of other's feelings with your own. Empathetic people feel the suffering of others so acutely that it can become troubling to and draining on that individual. If we become too distressed by what others are feeling and experiencing, we run low on mental and emotional resources and are no longer able to help that person or ourselves. Because the brain's neuro circuitry is adaptable, we can develop compassion and empathy for others the more we practice it.

Empathy appears to be an innate trait. Newborns exhibit a primitive form of empathy when they feel distress or cry in response to other infants crying. Studies show that children develop genuine empathy for others around the age of two.[126] Some research also suggests that women are more empathetic than men.[127] The saying declares, "Be kind, for everyone you meet is fighting a hard battle." Knowing that our brains are malleable, and empathy and compassion are important to connect with our fellow man, we must make it a priority to develop greater empathy and compassion.

With the risks and complications of organ donation, few acts are more heroic than donating an organ to a complete stranger. Like many in law enforcement, Officer Carolyn Becker of the Broomfield Police had a deep desire to serve her community, especially children, at a young age. After serving six years as a patrol and school resource officer, Becker saw an online post about a Broomfield High School student in need of a kidney. Without hesitation, the twenty-seven-year-old officer signed up to donate one of hers. Unfortunately, she was medically unable to donate a kidney because of her frequent kidney stones.

Disappointed but not defeated, she discovered the liver donation program and underwent all testing to find a positive match for one of many children waiting on Colorado's transplant-needs list. The testing revealed that she was a good match for an eleven-year-old boy whom she had never met, Clyde Hoffman. Hoffman was born with Alagille syndrome, a rare genetic disorder that primarily affects the liver and heart. Persons with this disorder have fewer bile ducts than normal causing excess bile to build up in the liver, resulting in liver damage.

So in August of 2018, she was admitted to the UCHealth University of Colorado Hospital in Aurora, where she experienced her first major surgery—removal of one-third of her liver. Her liver was successfully transplanted into Clyde, resulting in near-immediate improvement in his health.

As the Hoffmans focused on Clyde's recovery, Becker wasn't through with her compassionate generosity. She started a GoFundMe page to help cover the Hoffmans' medical expenses after she learned the surgery would leave them with more than $20,000 in debt. Between her personal efforts and the fundraising page, she raised roughly $11,000.

Becker exhibited remarkable compassion and altruism, explaining, "If I had a kid needing an organ, I'd be in a very desperate spot to see my kid healthy again. I felt like I could help," according to a Denver CBSN news report.[128]

Start with self-compassion. As stated earlier, most of us have harsh inner critics that have difficulty recognizing our own good. As long as we let this inner critic dominate us, we will find it hard to be compassionate toward others because of the pattern of self-abuse we have established that transfers to others.

Practice kindness not people pleasing. We should be kind to those around us, but it doesn't mean we have to give up who we are to appease others. People pleasing harms both the pleaser and the person being pleased. The pleaser alienates his true self and ultimately establishes a pattern of failing to meet his own needs. The person being pleased develops a feeling of entitlement and is barred from creating authentic relationships. Fake relationships will end when people pleasing does, but authentic relationships built on trust and true kindness endure.

Listen actively. Most people don't truly listen. We tend to interrupt and judge what others are saying, and much of our time in conversations is spent forming a rebuttal or the advice we want to give rather than actively listening. Active listening involves fully concentrating on what is being said. It makes the other person feel heard and valued. Active listening generally includes, nonjudgmental conversation, periods of silence, asking clarifying questions, reflecting back what you understood, verbal and nonverbal signs of listening (you need to actually look up from your phone and make eye contact), and summarizing what you learned from the conversation.

Seek to understand different perspectives. We use ourselves as the benchmark or standard by which we measure most everything. Our perspectives are shaped by our upbringings, educations, environments, and experiences, which are different from those of others. We may be convinced that our positions are absolutely right but so is the other person. Be genuinely curious about their conclusions and positions. Make your best effort to see the other person's perspective, which may lead to an improved conclusion for both of you.

Be fully present. Give people in your immediate presence the attention they deserve. Avoid glancing at the sports playing on the television behind your date or spouse at the restaurant, put your phone away, don't pay greater attention to the conversation next to you, and avoid distractions in general. Maintain eye contact and be engaged in the conversation at hand.

Examine your biases. We all have biases that impact our compassion. Our biases regularly lead to unconscious judgments about others. We tend to let our underlying attitudes and stereotypes determine whether or how we engage with others. Take opportunities to spend time with people of varying backgrounds. Recognize your similarities and respect differences.

Have uncomfortable conversations. No one likes to have their beliefs challenged by alternative points of view. However, respectfully discussing differing opinions develops character and allows us to show compassion for the opposition. Even when the other person's "truth" does not meet with reality, no amount of arguing and pressuring is going to change his or her mind. Quite the reverse, having courageous and respectful conversations with the opposition brings opportunity to come together. Acknowledge your emotions before participating in an uncomfortable conversation. Heightened emotions can interfere with active listening and thwart understanding. Be mindful that both of you are fallible human beings in the conversation. Be sure to separate ideologies from identity. Don't expect submission to your will and demand the other person change. The whole goal is to move from contempt and prejudice to appreciation and respect.

Unite in a shared cause. Despite how far apart two people seem to be from an ideological perspective, chances are you can find a cause both of you support. When you do find common ground, work together on that shared project. You may find that you develop a connection with and increase your compassion toward the other person as you work shoulder to shoulder.

We share the same rock (Earth) as our home, and it is in our best interest to make it the best place to live for each of us. Foster compassion and empathy in your life. We must gain a greater understanding of the issues humanity faces to solve the world's problems at an individual, local, national, and global level.

Compassion and empathy will guide us to decisions and solutions that meet the needs of humanity, not just ourselves. The tactics and strategies employed by the ruling elite lose power when we preserve a greater conviction to do what is ethical and moral for all of humanity because we genuinely care.

> Empathy begins with understanding life from another person's perspective. Nobody has an objective experience of reality. It's all through our own individual prisms.
>
> —Sterling K. Brown

CHAPTER 8

PERSISTENCE

When you have exhausted all possibilities, remember this, you haven't.

—Thomas Edison

Persistence is not giving up and tenaciousness in purpose. It is sticking to something even after momentum has slowed down or obstacles have impeded progress toward a goal. Persistence is a vital attitude and trait to develop because it is directly linked to your personal development, self-improvement, and success in life. It will take great persistence to regain humanity and break free from the ruling elite. They will not give up control easily, and many challenges and obstacles will need to be overcome to achieve the goal. Without persistence, defeat is inevitable.

Examples of persistence abound in successful individuals. Walt Disney was reportedly rejected 302 times before he obtained the financing to create Disneyland. Now six Disney parks dot the globe, representing his vision for creating a magical place for families to enjoy. Bestselling author John Grisham had his first book rejected twenty-eight times before he got a yes. Since then he has sold more than 250 million copies of his books. Similarly, Theodor Seuss Geisel, better known as Dr. Seuss, received twenty-seven rejections from publishers for his first book. Dr. Seuss later became one of the most renowned storytellers in history. Can you imagine *Indiana Jones* or *Star Wars* without Harrison Ford? Well, that could have happened if Ford had heeded the counsel he received from a Hollywood executive who said he would never succeed in the movie business. Thomas Edison was told as a child he was too stupid to learn anything, was fired from his first two jobs, and failed to create a working light bulb at least one thousand times. His persistence paid off with a successful lightbulb and more than a thousand patents, including many world-changing devices. Some only achieve success after they are gone. The famous painter Vincent Van Gogh only sold one single painting during his lifetime, yet now he is recognized as one of the greatest artists of all time. Could success be lurking around the corner for you if you persist? Absolutely! Persistence is a direct path to success, eventually.

You've probably heard that you only fail if you give up. Even the best, most well-thought-out plan and greatest preparedness is insufficient if you lack persistence. If things don't go according to plan, you will quit unless you develop a contingency plan to realize your goal. Plans intent on achieving something great will always require some level of adjustment. Roadblocks inevitably interfere, unknown factors arise, discouragement, and poor execution are just a few of the reasons why contingency plans are important. Thomas Carlyle said, "Permanence, perseverance, and persistence in spite of all obstacles, discouragements, uncertainty, and impossibilities: It is this, that in all things distinguishes the strong soul from the weak." The level of tenacity with which you relentlessly pursue your goals will determine victory or defeat.

Persistence can be applied to every aspect of your life: personal, professional, and casual. If you want to lose weight, you can't expect one day of better eating and activity to be the means to that end. Likewise, a successful business isn't going to bloom after just a weekend of effort. Improving your time to run a 5K also requires persistent practice and determination. Those who achieve great things have a killer determination and put in great efforts. Unfortunately, we usually only see their results rather than their tremendous efforts, which causes some to believe success came easy to them.

One of the greatest movie scenes of all time depicting persistence is the death crawl scene from *Facing the Giants*. Grant Taylor (Alex Kendrick) is a failing head football coach at Shiloh Christian Academy, with six straight losing seasons. After his seventh season starts out with a three-game losing streak, the player's parents want him fired, and his team is losing confidence. To top it all off, he is facing significant adversity in his personal life—leaking roof, infertility, appliances breaking down, and unreliable transportation.

Suffering through severe unrest, he turns to God through prayer and Scripture study. He implements a new coaching philosophy of praising God despite the game's outcome, and he encourages his players to give greater efforts, promising them they can win if they also turn to God. In a particularly poignant and inspiring scene, Taylor pushes team captain Jeremy Brock (Jason McLeod) further than he thought he could go.

Taylor asks Brock to do a death crawl to the fifty-yard line, which Brock thinks he can only do without a person on his back. A death crawl involves moving across the field from one end zone toward the other crawling on your hands and feet without knees touching the ground. To add to the difficulty, Brock must carry a 160-pound teammate on this back the whole way. Before Brock begins, Taylor places a blindfold on him so that he won't quit before he's given his very best efforts.

As Brock doubts that he can make it to the fifty-yard line and struggles with dwindling energy and endurance, Taylor continues to motivate and encourage him forward. He refuses to let Brock quit as he groans in pain and wants to give up. Not blindfolded, the rest of the team witnesses Brock's accomplishments as he collapses prostrate on the ground in the other end zone. His best was far beyond his own expectations and beliefs as he completed a hundred-yard death crawl across the field.

The scene served as a major turning point in the movie where Brock and the rest of the players learned to conquer fear, exercise faith in themselves and God, dig deep for strength they never knew they had, and persist toward the goal. Inspired with improved attitudes and renewed determination, the team goes on to win all the remaining games in their regular season and qualify for the state playoffs.

Another great story of persistence is the story of New Zealander Burt Munro—born Herbert James Munro—who fulfilled his decades-old dream to break land-speed world records. He embodied persistence as his life was in doubt from birth. He was born a twin, but his twin sister died at birth, and the doctors informed his parents that he would likely be dead before age two. He survived much longer than his doctors predicted, only to be stuck in work he didn't enjoy, farming. Growing up on his family's farm, Munro wished to see the world and pursue his passion for motorbikes. He often rode the family's fastest horse across the farm to feel the rush of speed, eventually riding motorcycles at age fifteen.

During his midtwenties, Munro started competing in motorcycle racing, including hill climbs, road racing, and drag racing. He upgraded two of his favorite bikes, an "Indian Scout" and a "Velocette MSS," with some advanced modifications, using unique parts like a Ford truck axle as the rods for his Indian bike. He also made his own parts and tools. After setting multiple land speed records in New Zealand, Munro set his sights on the Bonneville Salt Flats in Utah, USA, which is known for its flat, compacted salt, ideal for testing speed machines.

Munro's Indian Scout was an early model that had an original top speed of 55 mph (89 km/h) and a displacement of 600 cc. He significantly upgraded it to 950 cc and a top speed around 200 mph (321 km/h). With little time (he worked full-time as a motorcycle salesman) and money, he frequently worked overnight to modify his bikes, going to work on almost zero sleep. Munro realized his dream of going to the Salt Flats ten times, racing there nine times. He set three records there: 178.95 mph (287.99 km/h) in the 883-cc class, 168.07 mph (270.48 km/h) in the 1,000-cc class, and 183.59 mph (295.46 km/h) in an under-1,000-cc class. Munro also had an untimed and unofficial qualifying run that eclipsed 200 mph and a timed but unofficial run that reached 205.67 mph (330.99 km/h).

During all his adventures and success, Munro frequently corresponded with his friend and fellow motorcycle enthusiast John Andrews in England. Andrews described his letters as having no equal for determination, persistence, and ingenuity. Munro endured doubt and even a bit of resentment from his family initially and didn't let time, money, or distance keep him from achieving his dreams.

Developing persistence requires effort and practice. Many people set goals and make place for a triumphant achievement, yet very few actually succeed. Many quit before they even start, and a great majority of those who start don't stick to it until their goals and plans are fully accomplished. It is easier to relax and do nothing and stay within our comfort zones than to risk temporary setbacks and the discomfort of powering through whatever comes between us and our goals. Now is the time to develop your persistence.

Identify your goals. The first step of persistence is to determine what you want to accomplish. Write down your goals no matter how impossible they may seem to achieve. In Disney's *Alice in Wonderland*, Alice meets the Cheshire cat at a fork in the road. Not knowing which way to go, she asks the cat for directions. His shrewd answer is, "That depends a good deal on where you want to get to." Alice, being in unfamiliar territory and unsure of her goal, replies she doesn't really care where. Again, the Cheshire cat gives a wise answer, "Then it doesn't much matter which way you go." He was trying to help Alice understand that goals provide directions and help us determine paths in life. Without them, what paths and actions we choose matters very little.

Clarify your motivation. Motivation can be the difference between quitting and enduring. For example, if your motivation to lose weight is to please your boyfriend who wants you to look like the skinny models he sees in magazines, you probably will quit the first time you face adversity. However, if your motivation to lose weight is to be healthier so you can live longer and enjoy more quality years with your spouse, children, and grandchildren, you will likely have a loftier inspiration that leads to success. Know why you are doing what you are doing!

Model a successful person. Chances are someone has achieved what you want to achieve. That person has been through the process, conquered the obstacles, and redirected his or her plans until he or she realized the goal. Seek advice from a person who has achieved success in your desired area to gain valuable insights and guidance.

Create a plan. Outline how you will achieve your goal. The more definite and detailed your plan is, the more you will foresee potential obstacles. Research what it takes to do what you want and then implement a comprehensive plan to accomplish it. Don't forget to shape at least one contingency plan.

Maintain a positive attitude. Realize that temporary setbacks and adversity are bound to happen before goal achievement. No road to a worthy goal is easy. Temporary defeats and failures will derail you from the path you mapped out if you don't maintain a positive attitude and instead allow fear and doubt to cloud your mind.

Focus on the possibility. Focus on what's possible not the impossible. If you want to run a faster mile, set a reasonable but challenging goal. You would be unwise to set the goal of running the mile in 3:15 since the current world record set by an elite athlete is 3:43.13. Seeing the possibility helps maintain an optimistic attitude and hope. Develop a mindset where you focus on the results rather than the problems delaying your goals.

Surround yourself with a supportive tribe. You'll need people to help you reach your goal. Carefully select a group of people whom you trust and who have the skills and experience to assist you. Keep in mind that your tribe should consist only of people with positive mindsets who will provide you constructive criticism. Pessimistic and skeptical individuals will not help you succeed.

Be disciplined. Habits take time to change and form. Persistence will only become a habit if you develop discipline. Discipline brings stability and structure and teaches responsibility and respect. Discipline is taught in the military because it builds character and contributes to a cohesive team. Even if you lack some knowledge and experience to accomplish your goals, discipline can be the key to propel you forward. Life without discipline is like a plane flying through a storm without the proper instruments. Discipline provides direction, harmony, and order.

Reward yourself. Reward yourself when you complete a step toward your goal and make the reward big when you realize the total goal. Rewards can enhance motivation and commitment, giving you an edge to get the job done. Make the reward appropriate to your goal. For instance, it's probably not a good idea to allow yourself a week off your eating plan after you lose your first ten pounds of weight. However, a pedicure or a massage may be just the reward you need to keep going without sabotaging your goal.

Persistence is developed like your muscles. The more you exercise this trait, the stronger your persistence becomes. Perseverance habitually takes a back seat to genius and creativity, but neither genius nor creativity breed achievement without persistence. In other words, persistence trumps genius and creativity.

Determination and a refusal to quit lead to the underdog stories that become legend. Think David conquering Goliath, the 2007 defeat of Michigan by Appalachian State in American football, the "Miracle on Ice," or the Battle of Golan Heights. Indeed, perseverance is exactly what we need as we seek to regain humanity and take control from the elites because we are living a modern-day David-versus-Goliath moment.

> Ambition is the path to success. Persistence is the vehicle you arrive in.
>
> —Bill Bradley

CHAPTER 9

INCLUSION

We all should know that diversity makes for a rich tapestry, and we must understand that all the threads of the tapestry are equal in value no matter what their color.

—Maya Angelou

You've probably heard that variety is the spice of life, but could it be wrong, and diversity is the spice of life? Diversity makes life more interesting and enjoyable. It is good for creativity, innovation, and performance. Inclusion respects, embraces, and celebrates diversity in a meaningful and authentic way. It involves fostering an environment in which all individuals are treated fairly and have equal access to opportunities.

Diversity and inclusion are so frequently used together that they are often misunderstood to mean the same thing. However, diversity is simply a measure of the distribution of personal characteristics within a specific group of people. It is most often applied to race or gender, but this thinking is too narrow and doesn't capture the actual dimensions of diversity that are found in society. Diversity includes everything that contributes to making a person unique—gender, ethnicity, religious beliefs, culture, political beliefs, profession, socioeconomic background, sexual orientation, age, nationality, personality, family status, language, food choices, health, and more.

Inclusion, on the other hand, is significantly more important and includes deliberate actions to make each individual and group feel welcomed, valued, and supported. Diversity forces each individual to be assigned labels based on their characteristics and habitually places people in overly broad categories that lack actual commonality outside of one identifying characteristic. The very notion of diversity contributes to stereotyping by failing to see variances within groups of people classified only by a solitary characteristic. Indeed, many racial constructs depend on our natural inclination to sort things into groups. Another major shortcoming of overstressing diversity is the fact that it emphasizes differences rather than similarities. Inclusion is the answer to the problems of a short-sided focus on diversity. It underscores the value of harmony while maintaining individuality.

Antiracism activist Nova Reid summed it up concisely when she declared, "Diversity without inclusion is tokenism."[129] Tokenism is the policy of making only a symbolic effort toward providing equal opportunities to underrepresented groups in order to deflect criticism or appear virtuous. Mockingly, those who feign obsession and fervor for diversity are largely found at institutions of higher learning with the least diversity. Research reveals that the majority of college professors and teachers are liberal white men and women. Seventy-five percent of college faculty are white, and liberal professors outnumber conservatives twelve to one.[130,131] Their near-maniacal cry for diversity is classic do what I say, not what I do, and duplicitous at best. Authentic inclusion genuinely seeks to make opportunity and access equal for all. Notice that the imperative words are *equal opportunity* and *access*, not *outcome equality*. Outcome is determined by a multiplicity of factors, including your own personal efforts and determination.

Tokenism was on full display in April 2021 when Major League Baseball (MLB) chose to move their all-star game from Atlanta,

Georgia, to Denver, Colorado, in response to a new Georgia voting law. The main components of the Georgia law removes the Georgia secretary of state as the chair of the state elections board, grants greater oversight over county election officials, requires at least one drop box for absentee ballots in each Georgia county, expands early voting for primaries and general elections, shrinks the length of runoff campaigns from nine to four weeks, shortens the absentee ballot period from forty-nine days to twenty-nine days prior to an election, prevents sending unsolicited absentee ballots, and improves voter identification (ID) requirements—voters must provide their driver's license numbers, state ID card numbers, last four digits of their Social Security numbers, or a copy of a utility bill, bank statement, or government check. The voter ID requirement enhances vote integrity by replacing the less precise and subjective attempt to match signatures that was previously used. The provisions are meant to enhance election integrity and reduce voter fraud. In some ways, the Georgia voting bill expands voter access, and really, the most debatable aspect of the law is the controversial authority given to the state legislator.

MLB argued that the new law disproportionately affected minorities and limited voting access and, in response, moved their all-star game from Atlanta, which has 64.4 percent minorities (51.0 percent black)[132] to Denver, Colorado, which has only 48.4 percent minorities (9.8 percent black).[133] While it is true that minorities are slightly less likely to have a driver's license than white people, the ability to use various other forms of ID, including something virtually universal in utility bills, does not actually restrict voting access. Nearly three-quarters of US citizens want all voters to be required to show photo ID to vote.[134] An ID is required to purchase alcohol, board a plane, stay in a hotel, rent an apartment, open a bank account, apply for food stamps or welfare, get married, buy a cell phone, pick up a prescription, and more. IDs are practically ubiquitous in modern life. Ironically, the city MLB chose to move to, Denver, already has voter ID laws and allows for fewer early voting days than the new Georgia law permits. In addition, MLB requires voter ID to pick up tickets at Will Call, suggesting they recognize the need for valid ID to participate in certain aspects of society. The reality is MLB's tokenistic and hypocritical move of their game hurts minority-owned businesses in the Atlanta area and does nothing to improve voter access. If MLB really cared about minority access to voting, rather than just desiring to appear to care, they would engage in campaigns to help disenfranchised people get the necessary IDs or documents so they can vote.

Each of us is naturally inclined to favor people that look and act like us and judge other individuals according to patterns we see in ourselves and those we most closely associate with. Innate biases are developed based on these archetypes that influence the lens through which we see and accept others. However, having these innate biases does not make us inherently racist or bigoted. If so, every single human would be a racist or bigot. Instead, racism and bigotry are intentional acts. They involve purposefully intolerant attitudes that race, creed, opinion, or character accounts for the superiority of one group of people over another. It involves deliberate prejudice against a specific group of people.

Race and religion take the forefront of exclusionary attitudes and policies because these are the categories of people most often discriminated against. It may come as a surprise that Christianity is the most persecuted and discriminated against religion in the world, suffering persecution in 168 countries. According to a report for Civata UK, Christians are targeted—harassed, actively oppressed, and socially disadvantaged—more than any other body of believers.[135] Islam is the second most discriminated against religious group, with harassment experienced in 121 countries. Judaism is third, despite only one percent of the total world population practicing Judaism. Most of the worldwide population consider themselves a member of a specific religion, and many of these religions teach love of others. The prevalence of so much religious persecution in the world today, however, suggests that people say they're religious but don't actually practice the tenets their religions teach.

Discrimination comes primarily in three forms: direct, indirect, and intersectional. Direct discrimination involves the explicit categorization of groups of people to limit or remove that group's rights and opportunity. For instance, a policy at work that only women, not men, can be chief executives. Indirect discrimination is when a law, practice, or policy disproportionately disadvantages a specific group without explicitly mentioning this group. Maybe a minimum height requirement is set for a job where height is not relevant. Although it doesn't explicitly mention women, this policy could discriminate against them since they tend to be shorter than men, on average. When several forms of discrimination combine to leave a particular group at an even greater disadvantage, it is called intersectional discrimination. Discrimination occurs when a person or group of persons don't have equal access to human or legal rights because of an unjustified policy, law, or practice.

Few realize that slavery wasn't invented when the first enslaved people arrived in the United States from Africa in 1619. The history of slavery spans centuries and includes many cultures, nationalities, and even religions. We know the ancient Egyptians practiced slavery because Joseph of Egypt in the Bible was sold into slavery by his older brothers.[136] The Code of Hammurabi from the eighteenth century BC includes details of relationships and the medical treatment of slaves.[137] Forced labor and slavery were practiced in both the leading city-states of Greece, Sparta and Athens, during the seventh century BC.[138] Slavery with great brutality was employed widely by the Romans in the last two centuries BC. Kept mainly for work in households, offices, and armies, slavery continued from the sixth to the fifteenth centuries in the Mediterranean. So many Slavs (a European ethnolinguistic group) were captured and made slaves during the eastward expansion of the Germans in the tenth century that their name became the generic term *slave*. Even white European Christians were enslaved by Muslims in North Africa from 1530 to 1780. Today, slavery is still practiced in various forms from human trafficking to forced labor. The truth is that slavery, inhumane as it is, has been exercised throughout recorded history and serves a dark spot on humanity.

Racism is evil and needs to be utterly obliterated! All men are created equal, but not all are treated equal. This fact is not likely to ever change completely because of extreme views that don't represent most people in society. Cruel and ignorant individuals and racist groups exist, just like individuals and groups perpetrate crimes. The problem is that some people choose to overgeneralize and categorize all people of a specific race because of the actions of an individual, or individuals, within that race. A racist white individual randomly attacks an elderly black woman and the assumption is that all white people are racist white supremacists. A black individual uses a pistol to steal a white woman's purse, so it is assumed that all black people are violent criminals. If a dog bit your child, you wouldn't presume a universal fact that all dogs of that breed, or dogs in general, are vicious and a threat to children. Why do we allow ourselves to make these mass assumptions about people within specific groups based on individual acts? Racism may not be entirely defeated, but what we can work toward is equal opportunity. Part of this involves quenching the hyperbolic echo chamber into which today's politicians, professors, pundits, and common people shout their false narratives.

Spurious claims of systemic racism disregard the millions of individuals who are striving to practice inclusion and root out discriminatory practices. Real racism is practiced among the fringes of society and not by society at large to keep us divided. The reality is that most of the billions of people in society coexist peacefully with members of all races day in and day out. Still, racism is alive and well in the hearts of the few. Fortunately, research suggests that racist attitudes are further declining in modern society, particularly among the rising generations. A study reported that both conscious and unconscious racial and sexual-orientation bias declined significantly from 2007 to 2016.[139] It also revealed that unconscious bias may be largely generational. Unintended bias was identified most frequently among people who grew up when racial undertones were more prevalent—Baby Boomers and Gen Xers. Similarly, research from the University of Pennsylvania found that anti-black and anti-Hispanic prejudice declined sharply beginning early in 2016.[140] It is interesting to note that these notable declines occurred during the administration of two very different US presidents—Barack Obama and Donald Trump—suggesting that the sitting president has little influence on prejudice among his constituents.

Although the research is positive, Americans and others remain unaware of their own biases, and extremists seem more willing to openly express their prejudiced views. Other research suggests that racism is worse than most people are willing to acknowledge.[141] In addition, racial disparities exist in many facets of life, including employment, wealth, health care, the justice system, home ownership, and education.[142] Discrimination and prejudice remain complex problems that affect many people with significant implications for the health of both individuals and the globe as a whole. It's important to recognize that racism is not a natural or fixed phenomenon. Rather, it is the product of social and historical forces and subject to change. It's far past time that we be that change.

Indeed, the discrimination pendulum has swung the opposite direction in some ways. Former employees of Google sued the company, alleging that it took its diversity initiatives to the extreme, excluding qualified white men simply because they weren't female or minorities. These former employees charge that white males are disregarded for promotions and hiring to meet quotas mandated to recruiters who earn a bonus for hiring females and minorities at Google.[143] All qualifications equal, a minority or female is likely to be selected for a position over a white male in most cases.

Google isn't the only one getting things wrong despite good intentions. A whistleblower at Coca-Cola leaked screenshots of company racism training that seeks to shame white people into being "less white."[144] The screenshots reveal that Coca-Cola directs employees to a LinkedIn Learning series that reminds white people that being "less white" means being less oppressive and eschewing feelings that white people "are inherently superior." The training preaches that all white people are naturally oppressive and discriminatory. Imagine the uproar had the training instead instructed workers to "be less black" or "be less Latino." True inclusion involves everyone, not just minorities, and emphasizes fair equality of opportunity. An inclusive society chooses and progresses people based on their demonstrated skills, ability, knowledge, merit, and intangible value, not arbitrary factors like race and gender.

All races experience discrimination—Asians, blacks or African Americans, Native Americans, whites or caucasians, and so on. To what degree each experiences discrimination changes based on locale and the predominance of one race over another in that area. Persecution and discrimination against black Americans will be briefly discussed as an example. Despite the end of slavery in 1863, direct discrimination against black Americans was rampant in the US Southern states that lost the Civil War. These states actively passed laws to restrict rights and maintain the plantation system they were accustomed to pre-Civil War. The Thirteenth, Fourteenth, and Fifteenth Amendments to the US Constitution were passed by the Republican-controlled Congress—who opposed slavery—to limit discriminatory Southern state laws and provide black individuals equal protection under the law. Despite this, many US citizens maintained deeply held beliefs that whites were superior and treated black individuals accordingly.

Unfortunately, the US Supreme Court set these advancements of rights back in the Civil Rights Cases of 1883 and in Plessy v. Ferguson, which determined it was constitutional for individuals or businesses to deny equal access to all races and confirmed policies of separate-but-equal facilities espoused by Jim Crow laws. As the nineteenth century came to an end, many black Americans saw self-improvement, through education and vocational training, as the single greatest opportunity to escape discriminatory laws and practices. However, this is only true when equal access to education and training opportunities exist to uplift the black community. Access to educational opportunities was hardly equal at the end of the nineteenth century and even through much of the twentieth century. We need to acknowledge the failures and accomplishments of history, including those linked to racial equality. Accept our failures and learn from them so we don't repeat those failures. Slowly, through crucial events, black Americans started to gain equality in the United States:

- establishment of the NAACP (National Association for the Advancement of Colored People) in 1908
- foundation of the Universal Negro Improvement Association (UNIA) in 1914
- great migration of black Americans from the rural South to the urban North during the 1920s
- registration of more than three million black Americans during World War II, many of whom fought for freedom overseas
- Jackie Robinson making it to professional baseball in 1947
- landmark Brown v. Board of Education case that desegregated public schools
- courageous actions by Rosa Parks on the Montgomery Bus, black students from the Agricultural and Technical College in Greensboro, North Carolina, who sat down for

lunch at a whites-only diner, and the movement espoused by Dr. Martin Luther King Jr.

- Civil Rights Act of 1964 that granted the federal government more power to protect citizens against all forms of discrimination
- Voting Rights Act of 1965 that banned literacy tests as a requirement for voting and mandated federal oversight of voter registration to reduce racial voting disparities
- Fair Housing Act of 1968 that addressed racial discrimination in housing
- and more.

Although improved today, there is still much work to be done and barriers to be destroyed to improve racial equality. You can meaningfully help by advocating for the following:

Be introspective. Examine your own beliefs about people of different races. If you find yourself being prejudiced, ask yourself why. Then be willing to change. Seek out people of that race and get to know them to remove any biases entrenched in your subconscious mind.

Teach your children. Antiracism and antidiscrimination practices begin in the home. Talk to your children about what racism is, how it makes people feel, and how to identify it. Teach children to be socially accepting of differences and encourage them to play or hang out with a diverse group of friends.

End private, for-profit prisons. The United States represents just 5 percent of the world's population, but has 25 percent of the world's prisoners, thanks in part to for-profit prisons. Economic incentives in privatized prisons permit corporations to profit off the incarceration of others through prison labor or investments. Operators of private prisons have spent money to influence policies and elected officials in their favor. These profiteering prison systems make humans a commodity from which to make money, particularly black men who receive nearly 20 percent longer sentences than white men who commit similar crimes.[145] However, for-profit prisons are just one factor among many including criminal activity, judicial behavior, and legislated sentencing guidelines that contributes to this outcome.

Identify and discontinue norms, values, and practices that disadvantage a group. Look at institutions and evaluate any customs, standards, values, and practices that give one race an advantage over another. Once identified, make changes to increase inclusion and equal opportunity.

See something, say something. Racism and discrimination still exist today, among all generations and races. Inaction or failure to stand up against it when you see it is silent support. Adopt a zero-tolerance attitude against all forms of discrimination.

Recognize stereotypes in media. Music, movies, TV, books, magazines, social media, and internet sites may be sharing stereotypical images or messages about racial groups. Ask yourself how specific racial groups are being represented. Are they in a wide range of roles or typecast to specific roles? Are they always portrayed with certain attitudes, characteristics, or flaws? Media can contribute to inaccurate judgments about certain races.

Attend ethnic celebrations. A wonderful way to learn about other cultures and ethnic groups is to attend their celebrations. Invited to a quinceañera? Make it a priority to attend. Ask your ethnic friends what holidays and events they celebrate to learn more.

Imagine a world without hate. Cultivate love, not hate. Our world would see dramatic improvement if we simply ended all forms of hate. Ending hate can happen one person at a time.

Today, many black Americans remain in communities with the least opportunities for upward mobility. Unfortunately, this is not an accident and reflects both the deliberate and unintentional consequences of US policies. The disproportionately high concentration of black Americans in areas of the country that also had large populations of black Americans before the Civil War suggests historical conditions had enduring effects on the outcomes of black Americans.[146] Because black Americans today are far more likely to live in the South or urban Midwest, any economic policy that disadvantages the South or Midwest would unjustly affect black Americans.

Although many appalling policies directly designed to discriminate against black Americans have been outlawed, policies that indirectly disadvantage black Americans still exist today. Public schools with the most black students are underfunded, limiting opportunities to improve education and training. Black children tend to attend worse schools, in part because local tax and property laws prevent their parents from moving to more affluent neighborhoods with better schools. Interestingly, research shows that both black and white students perform worse in schools with a high density of black students.[147] This was particularly true among black males who were noted as the lowest academic achievers. Similarly, disparities exist among Scholastic Aptitude Test (SAT) scores used for college entrance (see table below).[148]

Sex and Race/Ethnicity	Total SAT Score
Asian	1223
White	1123
Mixed race	1101
All students	1068
Male	1076
Female	1061
Hispanic	990
Pacific Islander	986
Native (American/Alaskan)	949
Black	946

This has nothing to do with intelligence; only a prejudiced individual would believe that skin color directly correlates with intelligence. Nonetheless, it may identify cultural and household

122

differences. Asians, who perform best on the SAT, tend to live in two-parent households with reverence for education and strong encouragement of hard work. In other words, they had family and parent support and are encouraged to excel in life. Another factor is motivation. Sociologist Dr. Phil Mead, University of South Wales, showed that non-English speaking immigrants to Australia performed better in school, on average, than their native-born Australian peers.[149] Mead hypothesized this was because the immigrants were highly motivated to improve their lives. It makes sense since these individuals already took great risks to leave their native countries and seek prosperity in a foreign land. They have lived in very challenging circumstances and are motivated to do what it takes to improve their situation.

In 2019, black Americans experienced the highest poverty rate at 18.8 percent, which was a historic low since officials have tracked this statistic, and significantly lower than poverty rates between 30 and 40 percent in the 1960s.[150] For Hispanics, poverty rates were 15.7 percent, and Asians and Caucasians 7.3 percent. One of the reasons—a single piece in a complex and contested situation—is black Americans are often depicted as the products of forces beyond their control. Although some actions are determined by outside influences for which we have no control, our deliberate choices and actions have a greater impact on the outcomes of our life. For instance, let's say I buy a milkshake and place it between my legs to continuing driving and eating. During the course of my journey home, a person cuts me off, causing me to spill the shake all over myself and my vehicle. If I choose to curse the driver, flip him the bird, ram the back of his car with mine, and then fight with him in the street, was that caused by external factors or my own internal choices? The obvious answer is personal choices. My choices after the experience led to my wrongful actions and the likely outcome of spending a night in jail. Success, therefore, is largely a result of our own choices and actions, and it is up to each individual to make positive change happen in his or her life.

Some black children grow up in environments where few adults have taught them what a fruitful life looks like and how to achieve it. Among some black families, poverty has been a way of life for generations, making it difficult to break the cycle. Research suggests that the likelihood of economic success is conditional on achieving three middle-class norms: 1) graduate from high school, 2) maintain a full-time job or have a partner who does, and 3) delay childbearing until married and older than age twenty-one.[151] Sadly, black Americans are less likely to achieve these norms than their white peers.[152] Analyzing the data by race reveals that both black and white Americans who follow the three norms enter the middle class (incomes three to five times the federal poverty line) at about the same rate, but white Americans are more likely to realize the higher end of the middle class. A range of interrelated factors contributes to this fact, including the education system, job market, and family dynamics (such as unintended pregnancies and marriage). Nonetheless, the greatest variables leading to the escape of poverty—for all racial groups—remain a stable family structure (preferably a two-parent household), career-related training or education, and full-time workforce participation. Promotion of these benchmarks must be prioritized as individual and societal goals or self-oppression will remain a major obstacle to upward mobility in the black community. Without addressing these contributing factors to inequality, no meaningful progress can be made to level the height of the hurdles for all races.

Attributing inequality solely to the variable of racism essentially tells minorities that they are without opportunity because of an oppressive system. It reinforces racism by implying that skin color precludes prosperity and upward mobility. This oversimplified and incomplete thinking ignores observed realities. Experience shows that race alone does not determine upward mobility potential, rather upward mobility is determined by a cluster of social and human factors that affect Americans of all races equally.

For instance, a *New York Times* article declared that an enormous black-white wage gap has existed since the 1950s, claiming that black men earn only fifty-one cents for every dollar white men make.[153] However, fully evaluating the data shows that this wage gap disappears when factors such as age, education, training, math and verbal skills, and work history are accounted for. When comparing equal skilled, educated, and qualified black and white workers, black men earn identical wages (99.9 percent) as white men.[154] Similarly, black-white housing gaps vanish when racial groups are contrasted based on family structure, educational attainment, and workforce participation.[155] Educational attainment has a profound inverse relationship with poverty and inequality. Indeed, children raised in families in the lowest economic quintile who earn a college degree have an 84 percent chance of moving up the income ladder.[156] In other words, all races can realize the American dream if they achieve the three middle-class norms. Attempting to blame racism as the single greatest threat to economic mobility—like critical race theory does—not only ignores facts, but it undermines the very foundation of racial progress.

Retired Vanderbilt University professor Dr. Carol Swain discussed how success came to her, despite being poor, female, and black, because she made good decisions, received help from decent people, and achieved an education. She articulated how nearly anyone can improve their situation when she declared, "I think I was blessed in one crucial way: I was born in America, a true land of opportunity for anyone of any color or background. In this country, where you start your life does not determine where you end up. When I hear young blacks—or anyone, for that matter—talk about systemic racism, I don't know whether to laugh or cry. I want to laugh because it's such nonsense. I want to cry because I know it's pushing untold numbers of young blacks into a dead end of self-pity and despair. Instead of seizing the amazing opportunities America offers them, they seize an excuse to explain why they're not succeeding.... It was

125

only when exposed to academic theories of oppression in graduate school that I was informed that because I was black, poor, and female, I could never do what I had already accomplished." We need to instill attitudes of success through effort rather than hindering minorities by inculcating them with toxic messages that they are powerless to free themselves from the bondage of poverty because of systemic racism.

Lest one think that having black skin means you have no chance of upward mobility, several inspiring examples of poverty to prosperity can be found within the black community. Born to former slaves, Annie Malone is one of America's first and most prominent black businesswomen. Her parents died when she was young so she was raised by an older sister. Frequent illness caused her to drop out of high school. Armed by a love for hairstyles, Malone developed a chemical that could straighten black women's hair without damaging the scalp and hair follicles. She founded Poro College to teach people about black cosmetology. Through her college and business model, she created jobs for seventy-five thousand women and is recognized as the first black female millionaire in the United States.

Cosmas Maduka worked from the age of four and dropped out of elementary school to help his mother after his father died. At age seven, he served as an automotive apprentice under his uncle. Eventually working his way through the automobile business, he owned his own auto parts company with his brother and built a business empire with over twenty-six branches nationwide (Coscharis Group). Maduka made his first million at age twenty-four. His persistence and hard work has led to additional economic opportunities in technology, medicine, and beverage.

Born in Somalia, Iman Abdulmajid moved to the land of opportunity to pursue a modeling career. Not only did she achieve her dream of becoming a model, but Abdulmajid also rose to become a successful business executive in the 1990s with her own cosmetics line. She also had a brief stint in acting. She transformed fashion and modeling and broadened the definition of beauty throughout her career. Abdulmajid is a classic example of overcoming challenges, enduring a taxi accident that paused her career and a divorce. She merges beauty and brains flawlessly and is well-known for her charity work.

Growing up in Port Elizabeth, South Africa, Lebo Gunguluza set a goal to become a millionaire by age twenty-five. He had to adjust his goal but did become a millionaire and one of South Africa's youngest self-made black millionaires by working in advertising until he became an entrepreneur and motivational speaker. This self-made millionaire has lost his fortune twice, but his relentlessness gained it back both times.

Actress Halle Berry spent the first few years of her life living in an inner-city neighborhood. Berry's father abandoned his wife and children when she was very young, prompting a move to a predominantly white suburb in Cleveland, Ohio. Here she was subjected to discrimination and racism that she used to enhance her motivation to excel in life. Berry moved to Chicago at age twenty-one to pursue her dream of becoming an actress. However, she quickly ran out of money and spent some time in a homeless shelter until she got her break. An acclaimed actress and former beauty queen, Berry is known for her prominent roles in *The Call, Boomerang, Die Another Day, X-Men*, and *Monster's Ball*.

Dr. Ben Carson—in full, Benjamin Solomon Carson Sr.—was born in Detroit in 1951. His parents divorced when he was just eight years old, making him a product of a single-parent household. Carson performed poorly during his early school years until his mother supplemented his regular schoolwork with additional reading and writing assignments. Driven by his newfound love of learning, he earned a scholarship to Yale University, where he earned a bachelor's degree in psychology. He furthered his education with a medical degree from the University of Michigan and completed his neurosurgical residency at Johns Hopkins University. He was the first surgeon to successfully separate conjoined twins attached at the back of the head and also refined a technique known as *hemispherectomy*—a procedure where one-half of the brain is removed to prevent seizures in people with severe epilepsy. After retiring as a surgeon in 2013, Carson became active in politics and served as US secretary of housing and urban development.

These are just a few of the many individuals in the black community who wanted a different life and pursued it until it became reality. Talking about and celebrating success stories from the black community need to become more prominent among black communities and the world as a whole.

Choose a goal and define a precise path to that goal. The choices each of us makes determine our destinies, not the color of our skin. There are obstacles in the form of prejudice, both perceived and real, but ultimately you control your own destiny. Assigning blame to other people or institutions to absolve oneself of poor decisions will not solve problems, nor does it lead to life improvement. Small acts of discipline build character and increase the likelihood of success. Pattern your life after successful individuals. Use them as a guide to help you make the right choices that will steer you away from hazardous detours. Don't let self-defeat cloud your vision, derail your aspirations, smother your dreams, and impair your life. Candace Owens said, "Racism exists, but it is far less rampant than ignorance, and ignorance can be cured through experience." A host of excuses, many of which come from your subconscious, will tell you that you can't do it, but you can! Believe in yourself.

Challenges for minorities will come up, so the question becomes what are we going to do to improve opportunity and upward mobility for our brothers and sisters? We must commit to make the hurdles equal in height for all races in America and the rest of the world. The book *Fish in a Tree* by Lynda Mullaly Hunt teaches us that everyone has value—it just takes more work to discover in some. The premise of the book is summarized in the statement that "everybody is a genius. But if you judge a fish by its ability to climb a tree, it will live its whole life believing that it is stupid." A fish can swim superbly, but it has no ability to climb a tree. This allegorical framework teaches us that it is inappropriate to judge people by focusing on a skill that they don't possess. People should be placed in environments where their genius and skills will shine and thrive.

Stable work, whether self-employed or employed, is the greatest escape from poverty. According to US census data, only 2.4 percent of people who work full-time and year-round live in poverty. On the contrary, that number climbs to 14 percent among people who work part-time and not year-round, and all the way to 32 percent among individuals who don't work.[157] Clearly, the best way to reduce poverty is increase the number of individuals working full-time and year-round. We need to implement comprehensive work support and training programs. Helping our neighbors obtain job training, land stable jobs, and earn wages and position increases over time is the most straightforward way to fight poverty.

In addition, improving housing is an important initiative. Public housing is frequently built in high-poverty areas so that they are close to the people who need them. However, this just concentrates people living in poverty in a single area. Building public housing in low-poverty areas could change this dynamic and provide hope for a better future.

School choice is another critical element to lifting people out of poverty. Children shouldn't be forced to attend failing schools just because their parents can't afford to move to a better area with better schools. Charter schools could be built, vouchers provided—including public transportation passes—for children living in poverty to attend more suitable schools. No single policy will correct the problems black Americans and other minorities face, but each one implemented and sustained will contribute to improving their upward mobility.

Inclusion permits opportunities to learn from different perspectives. People from different backgrounds can provide unique insights into the common struggles, experiences, and goals we each share. In addition, looking at the world through the lens of another person enlarges your understanding of the world. It may even prompt breakthrough thinking that changes your opinion on certain issues.

Bigotry, discrimination, and exclusion are the result of ignorance and programming. Most people don't willfully discriminate unless they were taught to do so by a trusted or authoritative individual. Despite this, we may unconsciously disregard people who are different from us because of embedded preconceptions. By becoming aware of our unconscious biases through honest self-examination, we can create an environment that is more inclusive.

Gaining insights into the motivations and dreams of others opens the doorway for kindness and understanding. Engage in meaningful conversations with people of diverse backgrounds. Get to know their families, work, views, and aspirations. Doing so increases familiarity and understanding and discovers commonalities. Perceptions and assumptions are often unfair and very dangerous. Chances are you'll find you have more in common than dissimilar, minimizing the effect these differences have in your relationships with people of other races. On subjects where you hold deep convictions, agree to disagree when necessary, without being disagreeable. Courageous conversations like this also reduce misconceptions and increase genuine compassion for others.

It really is unconscionable that we must discuss discrimination in the modern era. One would think that we as humans have developed as a society enough to move past practicing exclusion based on diversity. Today, it's virtually impossible to avoid interacting with others outside our self-defined groups. We encounter diversity at the grocery store, entertainment and sports venues, restaurants, workplace, schools, religious institutions, and various other organizations. The internet grants us unprecedented access to diversity all over the world. Candidly, we have no choice but to embrace our global connection to diversity and celebrate ourselves as citizens of the world while maintaining our national identity. Inclusion doesn't mean we become a melting pot that is unable to maintain deep-seated links to nationality and other defining characteristics. What it does mean is that we as humanity stand to benefit most if we learn to live inclusively with people who are different from us.

Unfortunately, some confuse inclusion with conformity and compliance. Compliance is acquiescing readily to others, especially in a subservient way. Both involve changing your behavior to fit in with a group or obey an authoritarian figure. People conform to expectations based on their social role and look to the group for direction. Unfortunately, conformity often leads to a phenomenon known as groupthink, where group members value coherence among the group above critical thought.

Groupthink occurs when well-meaning individuals make illogical and poor decisions because of a desire to conform to a particular belief. People stuck in groupthink refrain from expressing doubts or disagreeing with consensus even when the group decision is contrary to their moral values or ethics. Groupthink is dangerous because decisions are made to prioritize a specific goal or ideology while ignoring critical information, principles, and tenets. Conformity and inclusion are not the same and, indeed, harm diversity.

Too many wars have been fought and people shunned or killed because of fear and hatred espoused by groups of people who consider themselves superior to others. Rights have been denied and atrocities committed in the name of this superiority complex throughout history. Arrogance and ignorance prohibit understanding, trust, and willing communication from breaking down these fabricated barriers and bridging our differences.

The parable of the Good Samaritan in the Bible (Luke 10:25–37) teaches us how to love, serve, and be compassionate toward our neighbors, but some fail to recognize it is also a story of inclusion. To understand why, we need to understand who the Samaritans were. Samaritans were a mixed group of people descended from foreign occupiers of Israel (placed in Samaria by kings of Assyria and Babylonia after the captivity of the northern kingdom of Israel) and Israelites who escaped at the time of captivity. They were therefore partly Israelite and partly gentile. Rejected and hated by the Jews, great animosity developed between the two ancient peoples, so much so that hostility between the groups caused Jews traveling from Judea to Galilee or the other way to go out of their way and cross the river Jordan to avoid Samaria.

When the Jew traveling the road from Jerusalem to Jericho was beaten, robbed, and left half dead along the roadside, two Jews— a Jewish priest and a temple worker—failed to offer aid to their fellow countryman. Contrarily, a Samaritan put aside his feelings for the Jews and administered aid to him. He even paid for his future care. It would have been far more convenient for the Samaritan to allow the injured man to die on the road to Jericho, especially since he was considered an enemy. However, the parable is meant to teach us more than love, service, and compassion. By making the hero of the parable a Samaritan, not another Jew, Jesus teaches us we should love, respect, and serve everyone, even those with substantial differences and with whom we vehemently disagree. If we practice genuine inclusion, we will always reach out to all our neighbors, most importantly during times of need.

One caution is to not overemphasize equality or diversity at the expense of freedom and prosperity. There is a significant push today to choose people or organizations purely based on race or gender—a form of racism and discrimination itself. American economist Milton Friedman stated, "A society that puts equality before freedom will get neither. A society that puts freedom before equality will get a high degree of both." For instance, a business that overemphasizes the recruitment of minorities instead of hiring solely based on qualifications may find they are soon underperforming and no longer competitive. Diversity for diversity's sake is discrimination. Similarly, you probably wouldn't want a female doctor to operate on your heart whose specialty is podiatry just because she is female. The outcome would likely be death in this situation because she is not qualified to perform heart surgery. Nor should you vote for a candidate purely because they have the same skin color or are the same gender as you—this is a bigoted and unreasonable approach. Votes should always be cast for the candidate who holds values and espouses policies that most closely align with our own, regardless of race or gender. Doing so avoids divisive identity politics and considers a person's character more important than their gender or skin color. Attitudes and actions that make selections solely based on gender or race are disingenuous, discriminatory, and dangerous.

We really need each other. The old need the young for physical help. The young require the wisdom of the old. People from different walks of life and with diverse backgrounds need each other to fully appreciate humanity in all its variety. We need to lock arms and build a better world for our children and grandchildren and those who come after them. This will best be accomplished by practicing inclusion.

Be an example of inclusion at home, at work, and in all places. This is particularly important at home. As stated previously, people often learn discrimination from a trusted individual. Children can also adopt a mindset of inclusion if their parents model and teach it at home. There are many children's books that teach inclusion as well—*The Name Jar, Whoever You Are, Brontorina,* and *Strictly No Elephants*, to name a few. Your actions at work to include marginalized individuals could encourage others to do the same. When confronted with discriminatory actions, stand up against them and let it be known that you won't tolerate it. One brave act could redirect individuals, organizations, and communities.

We live in a time of considerable divisiveness. This divisiveness is fueled by the actions of the global elites who stir up contention solely to increase their wealth and power. We are naturally inclined to gravitate toward people who share similar attributes, partly because we fear being judged or misunderstood by those we perceive as not sharing our same values and characteristics. It takes courage to overcome these tendencies. Nevertheless, humanity needs people to take these risks so that we can unite around the richness and diversity present on Earth. We need to strive to be of one heart and mind when it comes to humanity. Foster a culture of inclusion. Only through greater harmony will we see less strife and contention and unite to improve the world for all human beings.

> Perfect love is to feeling what perfect white is to color. Many think that white is the absence of color. It is not. It is the inclusion of all color. White is every other color that exists, combined. So, too, is love not the absence of an emotion (hatred, anger, lust, jealousy, covetousness), but the summation of all feeling. It is the sum total. The aggregate amount. The everything.
>
> —Neale Donald Walsch

CHAPTER 10

RESPECT

> Respect is one of life's greatest treasures. I mean, what does it all add up to if you don't have that?
>
> —Marilyn Monroe

Respect is to feel or show admiration and regard for someone or something that you believe possesses good qualities. As a foundation of humane and ethical behavior, respect is a fundamental trait of ethical society. If you respect your neighbor's property and life, the world becomes a safer place. As children, we are taught to respect elders, teachers, law enforcement, cultural traditions, our country's flag, and so forth. When we are adults, we gain respect for exemplary individuals and lose respect for people we discover character shortcomings in. Respect acknowledges the existence, value, and accomplishments of others. It invites kindness and encourages you to treat others in a compassionate and friendly manner.

Respect for others begins with self-respect—a proper regard for one's own person and character; behaving with dignity and grace. Indeed, self-respect is the footing upon which life's decisions are made, how you treat others, and how you allow others to treat you. The respect we afford ourselves teaches others how to treat us.

Self-respect is often confused with self-esteem. Self-esteem is confidence in your abilities to perform well in the world. Self-respect, instead, is a deeper inner feeling that we can conduct ourselves with honor, integrity, and goodness. In short, self-esteem involves how you value your skills and abilities, whereas self-respect deals with the positive values you attribute to yourself. When you recognize your positive attributes—integrity, humility, kindness, and so on— you are less likely to be influenced by external factors, like the opinions of others.

Confucius profoundly stated that "without feelings of respect, what is there to distinguish men from beasts?" Respect means that you accept others for who they are, even when they are significantly different or you don't agree with them. A general lack of respect is on full display on social media and the internet. Hiding behind avatars and disconnected from human connection, people become keyboard warriors who indiscriminately type assaults and mean words. They are hell-bent on being right and persuading others to think the same way they do. Intolerance is the standard and conformity the goal. Keyboard warriors say things they would not say in face-to-face conversations because there is no fear of being punched in the proverbial face.

Lacking common decency, conversations have lost mutual respect. Mutual respect involves acknowledging differences, understanding their significance, and then creating an environment in which everyone feels welcomed, heard, supported, and fairly treated. Prioritizing mutual respect means responding to differences with interest, politeness, and care rather than dismissive rudeness and disparagement.

Even the most accomplished individual is seen in a negative light if they lack respect for others. "Being brilliant is no great feat if you respect nothing," German poet, playwright, novelist, scientist, and statesman Johann Wolfgang von Goethe said. Without respect your relationships suffer. It is difficult to love family, honor friends, believe your boss, or work with colleagues who've lost your respect. Lack of respect leads to lack of trust and a damaged, if even salvageable, relationship.

A nurse, humanitarian, and spy, Edith Louisa Cavell displayed not only great courage but respect in her life. Born in Swardeston, England, the religious faith that she was raised in significantly influenced her life. Trained as a nurse at the London Hospital in 1900, Cavell started one of the first nursing journals, *L'infirmiere*, which documented good nursing practices and standards. She taught nursing in different hospitals throughout Belgium, improving nursing standards of care.

Cavell was living in England when World War I broke out in 1914, but moved back to Belgium and the hospital she was familiar with. That hospital was later taken over by the Red Cross. Late in 1914, the Germans invaded Belgium, and Brussels was under stringent German military occupation. Unfortunately, many British soldiers were left behind in Brussels as Allied forces withdrew from the city.

Demonstrating respect for life and humanity, Cavell aided British servicemen by hiding them in the hospital and safe houses. Eventually, she facilitated the escape of around two hundred servicemen to neutral Holland. Even greater respect was shown when she treated wounded soldiers from both German and Allied forces. This was despite the fact that occupying German forces threatened severe punishment for any person caught aiding or abetting Allied forces.

By mid-1915, Cavell was under suspicion of aiding Allied forces and arrested. She did not attempt to defend herself after capture, maintaining that she did what was right by helping people in need. A short trial conducted by the German military tribunal found her guilty of treason and sentenced her to death. Despite pleas from US and Spanish diplomats, Cavell was executed. Just prior to her execution, Reverend Stirling Gahan, an Anglican chaplain, visited her and documented her last words, which included, "Patriotism is not enough. I must have no hatred or bitterness to anyone." Her legacy is that of having compassion and respect for people, even those we don't agree with.

Respect can be developed and fine-tuned. Developing greater respect and putting it into practice can help you be more successful.

Listen intently. Respect begins with listening intently. This seems like it would be a no-brainer, but unfortunately, people choose not to listen to conversations all of the time. Be present for the conversation and truly seek to understand not only what the person is verbalizing, but also what he or she is saying with body language, tone, and emotions.

Affirm. Affirming involves observing something positive about a person and verbalizing it. Many managers find it helpful to begin a conversation that involves admonishment with an affirmation. For instance, "You have shown a great deal of dedication to organizing the client files." Affirming someone shows that you respect and value them and recognize their positive contributions.

Be kind and polite. Treat everyone with kindness and be polite even if they don't reciprocate these behaviors. Kindness is a symbol of respect. It is marked by a pleasant disposition, ethical behavior, and genuine concern and consideration for others. Politeness is declining rapidly in today's society. People are rude on the roads, no longer hold the door for others, bad-mannered on the athletic field, and engage in rude discourse online. A simple act of politeness can change a person's day and inspire them to pay it forward to others. It really doesn't cost anything to be kind and polite, so make them a daily habit.

Use manners. Say please, thank you, and excuse me. Showing good manners reveals that you respect others.

Be helpful. We are meant to serve one another. Each of us possesses a unique set of skills and knowledge that allows us to help each other. You may know how to install brakes on a car, while your neighbor can prune fruit trees. You may be an expert bread maker, whereas your sister is good with computers. Each of these situations seems like a good way to swap expertise and serve one another. Be an asset to people and give more than you take.

Uplift. Think before you speak: Is it kind? Is it helpful? Is it true? If it isn't, then it is probably better left unsaid. With all our own critical self-talk, it is helpful to hear encouraging comments from those around us. Snide remarks don't belong in life. Always strive to introduce positivity into your interactions and seek to uplift others with your words. Remember to be sincere in your uplifting words. Disingenuous and artificial praise can be seen through and helps no one.

Accept your respect may be applied unevenly. Everyone deserves kindness and respect, but to what degree? You will find, and it is okay, that you respect some people more than others. For example, most of us would show greater respect to our grandmas by ensuring they have comfortable chairs while visiting our homes, even if it meant showing less respect for our kids by asking them to sit on the floor. Similarly, a consistently honest person will receive greater respect than a habitual liar.

Showing respect for others gives value to their beliefs and ideals. To stop the fighting among ourselves, which hostility only benefits the ruling elites, we need to prioritize and return to respect in all we do. We will never agree on every topic—nor should you adopt a viewpoint that you don't agree with because you feel forced to by others—but each of us should be free to express our views. From there, it is up to us to accept or reject those viewpoints after carefully listening to the other person. Practicing respect for all humanity is central to a thriving society and vital to detaching from the ruling elite's programming.

> I speak to everyone the same way, whether he is
> the garbage man or the president of the university.
>
> —Albert Einstein

CHAPTER 11

HUMILITY

Humility is not thinking less of yourself, it's thinking of yourself less.

—C. S. Lewis

Humility is the state of being modest and free of pride and arrogance. The language root of humility comes from the Latin word *humulitas*, derived from *humus*, which means "from the earth." Using this root, humility is therefore grounding, permitting us to improve our ability to identify what is important in life. It is an attitude of recognizing our places in the world and a clear appreciation for the strengths, importance, and viewpoints of others. It includes genuine listening to see things from the perspective of others. Humility is a virtue that places everyone on a level playing field.

Humility seems counterintuitive because we are taught to have self-esteem and confidence in our abilities and accomplishments. Look at the confidence displayed in successful businessmen, athletes, and world leaders. One may think confidence is far more important than humility based on these standards. However, humility isn't denial of your accomplishments and abilities, but rather not placing too much weight on their significance.

The essence of humility is being mindful that without the contributions of many others, you would not have achieved success. The way your parents raised you, family guidance, the influence of teachers from grade school on up, challenges you have overcome, skills acquired through work, official and unofficial mentors, and meaningful opportunities each impact our success. A multiplicity of factors and defining moments shaped you into the person you are now and enabled you to achieve.

Despite what some may think, humility has nothing to do with weakness or submissiveness. Instead, it acknowledges the value and contributions of others, our weaknesses, and our need for continual growth and learning. Arrogant individuals believe they already know everything and have all the skills they need to succeed. By taking this approach, their competence deteriorates. Humble people, on the other hand, constantly seek to absorb new knowledge from others and acquire new skills.

Humble people are more teachable. Humility acknowledges errors and fixes them. By recognizing that you have much to learn, you become open to mentorship that leads to greater success. No one individual can be well-informed about every subject. That is why two heads are better than one—they unite their individual brilliance to form collective genius.

Another myth about humility is that it causes us to lower our value in comparison to others. Humility is really about recognizing others as equals. Saying something kind to build up another person or celebrating their accomplishments in no way diminishes your own merits or value. Unfortunately, people who rise to positions of power often attempt to sabotage rising leaders to protect their own statuses. They feel threatened and insecure because of the talents of others. Nevertheless, humble leaders empower and mentor others to rise to their full potentials. If you possess true humility, you won't worry about others surpassing you—you are happy when you help others be the best possible version of themselves.

Digressing for a moment, we are all created equal, endowed with divine potential. With few exceptions, putting gender, race, sexual orientation, or religion in front of a person's achievements is reductive and can belittle their accomplishment. By placing these qualifiers in front of accomplishments, we essentially place them in a different and unequal competitive category. Doing so is a tactic to perpetuate identity politics and the us-versus-them mentality.

You'd think that confident leaders are the most successful, but this is not always the case. Sure, confidence is important, but humble confidence—sometimes called servant leadership—is more important. Humble leaders—those who admit mistakes, highlight the strengths and contributions of team members, solicit feedback, and model being teachable—are better liked and more effective.[158] Humility leads to higher team performance, improved collaboration, and greater flexibility.[159] Humble leadership consequently advances organizational performance.

People who are humble not only make better business leaders but also make better employees. A survey of supervisors discovered that employees that were perceived as honest and humble received higher ratings of overall job performance.[160] These findings make perfect sense, because humble employees are more teachable and willing to accept correction that would ultimately lead to improved performance.

Not surprisingly, the same trait of humility can make you a better student in school. Researchers evaluated the impact of humility among college students as part of two separate experiments.[161] Researchers found that not only did humble students possessed desirable traits like self-esteem, gratitude, and forgiveness, but also they got better grades.

It takes humility to admit you were wrong, say sorry even when you are not wrong, and forgive. Virtually any relationship will involve times when you are hurt or offended by another person. Researchers sought to determine the role of humility in repairing strained relationships.[162] During the first experiment, college students in a romantic relationship who had been hurt or offended

143

by their partners in the last two months were included. The participants documented measures of humility and forgiveness for six consecutive weeks. As part of the second experiment, college students were placed in small groups that completed tasks intended to challenge humility. Strong social bonds were strengthened, and relationships repaired through humility. In both experiments, humility proved a highly valuable trait for positive relationships.

Humility decreases anxiety. People who are humble embrace their true selves and are less hyperfocused on how others see them. Anxiety partly stems from the fear that people will not like our true selves. Reality shows that some people will not like you, but it doesn't mean you are an awful person. Others may not like you because you chose to give money to a homeless person, intervened when a member of the LGBT community was being shamed, or stood up when a person of color was excluded from a community organization. In each of these situations, you chose the right in a hard situation at your own personal detriment. You'll never please everyone, nor can you be a person who everyone will like. Humility helps you overcome fear, worry, and anxiety.

Humility decreases feelings of entitlement and prejudice. It is far better to be grateful for what you've earned than to feel entitled to what others have worked for. Humble people don't feel like they are owed what others possess. Instead, humility fosters desires of equality and inclusion. A series of four studies found that practicing humility promotes desires for social equality and diminishes stereotyping and prejudices against people who are different from us.[163] Humility removes the about-me attitude that clouds our worldviews and causes us to consider the needs of others.

When comparing humble people to conceited people, humble people are more willing to help others. A sequence of three studies measured a person's willingness to help others in correlation with their self-reported level of humility.[164] The researchers reported that humble people displayed altruistic behaviors and were more willing to help others when an unexpected opportunity for service occurred.

The greatest leaders in history balanced unmistakable confidence with resounding humility. Uruguayan politician José Alberto Mujica Cordano, José Mujica for short, served as the fortieth president of Uruguay from 2010 to 2015. Born to parents of modest means, Mujica joined the Tupamaro, a revolutionary organization established to undermine Uruguay's repressive leadership. He was arrested several times for his involvement in violent activities associated with Tupamaro, including killing a police officer in 1971. As a prisoner, Mujica was tortured and confined to solitary for long periods, including two years at the bottom of a well.

Amid an increasing economic crisis and demands for democracy, the brutal military dictatorship negotiated a return to a democratic government in 1985. Political prisoners, like Mujica, were released as part of a general amnesty deal later that year. The Tupamaro joined the Broad Front and organized as a legitimate legal party in preparation for the 1989 elections, and Mujica rose to become one the most vocal leaders of the new party.

Mujica served one term in the chamber of representatives before being elected to the Senate in 2000 and again in 2004. He also served as minister of agriculture under President Tabaré Vázquez from 2005 to 2008. Riding the popularity and success of Vázquez, Mujica won nomination as a presidential candidate in 2009. Danilo Astori, one of his chief competitors, joined his ticket as the vice-presidential candidate. However, his guerilla past and public criticism of leaders of other South American leaders, like Argentina and Venezuela, stimulated controversy. Mujica defeated former president Luis Lacalle Herrera after a runoff and took office March 1, 2010.

Uruguay thrived under Mujica's leadership, experiencing low unemployment rates and consistent GDP growth. The economic prosperity under Mujica resulted in improved public services in health and education. He radically changed social policies in Uruguay. For instance, he legalized marijuana to limit profits of drug dealers, maintaining that drug dealing was the real problem, not consumption of cannabis. While not everything he did was exemplary, he lived a life of humility.

Mujica was dubbed the "world's poorest president" because of the humble circumstances he embraced. He accused rich societies of overconsumption, waste, and blind obsession to accumulate wealth. He donated 90 percent of his salary to charity, shunned the lavish presidential palace for a farmhouse, and for the longest time, a 1987 Volkswagen Beetle was his only asset.

Humility requires practice. Consider following these tips to develop more humility.

Listen well. Listening seems to come up time and time again in developing these positive characteristics, and for good reason. We have two ears and one mouth, suggesting we should listen twice as much as we speak. Remember you aren't listening when you are speaking. Genuine listening demonstrates high regard for others.

Never stop learning. Albert Einstein reportedly said, "Once you stop learning, you start dying." There is always something new to learn, and you're never too old to gain further knowledge or acquire a new skill. Establish quality relationships with people who can mentor you, formally or informally. Information is readily available today at the click of a mouse, so there are no excuses for not making learning a lifelong process.

Admit and correct mistakes. We all make mistakes. They are unavoidable. The key is to learn from the mistake, correct it, and reduce the likelihood of making the same mistake in the future.

Mature individuals admit their responsibility for their imperfect decisions and actions, accept the consequences, and make mistakes a lesson and opportunity for personal growth.

Be grateful not boastful. There is a difference between expressing gratitude for your blessings and accomplishments and ensuring everyone knows about it. Remember: you couldn't have achieved your goal without the help of countless individuals and experiences. If you have achieved something great, people will already notice it, no need to brag about it. Boasting is an attempt to prove you are above others.

Appreciate others. Congratulate others for their achievements, even if they outperformed you. Compliment people for good work. Keep in mind that appreciating someone does not make you less important or inferior. Express sincere appreciation generously, even for small things or matters that you feel the other person is obligated to do for you. All moms like hearing, "This dinner was delicious, thank you," even though children believe moms are obligated to cook the family meal.

Be patient with others. No one wakes up in the morning and says, "I'm going to mess everything up today." Recognize that each person is doing the best he or she can with what that person has. People will make mistakes, offend us, and be unjust from time to time. Our first reaction is probably to react emotionally and seek retribution. Yet patiently responding to the unjust and misguided words or actions of others demonstrates strength of character and provides an opportunity to practice humility.

Accept a lowly place. Try not to be offended when others receive recognition or honor for something you expected (e.g., employee of the year or a promotion). We don't always get the seats of honor or the recognition we deserve. Christ was born in a shelter for animals, and his bed was a manger, yet He was the greatest person to ever live on this earth. Humbly accept your current circumstance and diligently work to improve.

Humility is liberating and empowering. It enables us to be better wives and husbands, parents, sons or daughters, neighbors, friends, and coworkers. Humility has the potential to solve many of our most pressing socioeconomic issues and global challenges. Humility leads to greater humanity. We must each strive to be humble to remove prejudices, appreciate other's perspectives, and regain our humanity regardless of pressure to remain separate.

> Every person that you meet knows something you don't; learn from them.
>
> —H. Jackson Brown Jr.

CHAPTER 12

HOPE

> Hope itself is like a star—not to be seen in the sunshine of prosperity, and only to be discovered in the night of adversity.
>
> —Charles Haddon Spurgeon

Hope—desire or confidence for something to be true or good things to happen—is a vital trait for humans to possess. It makes tough situations bearable and propels you to take steps to improve your life. Hope provides a feeling of control over one's life. It is confidence that we can overcome adversity as we seek to reach a worthy objective. It is seeing opportunities during hardship, believing in a positive future, and seeing the plus side of situations.

Hope and optimism are not the same; rather, optimism is a level on the spectrum of hope. Hope requires planning and work, while optimism is simply a positive thought pattern. Both optimists and pessimists have hope at varying levels on the spectrum of hope. Optimism is a greater degree of hope, whereas pessimism hangs onto very little hope. From a spiritual point of view, hope is exercising faith in a higher power that things will work out for your good.

Hope is not blindly believing that good things will appear out of the ether simply because you wish for them. Nor is it false, where you believe you will avoid harm after intentionally choosing a dangerous situation. For instance, it isn't hoping your broken leg will set itself and heal without proper medical attention. Similarly, it isn't quitting your job because you hope you will win the lottery and be able to subsist on the winnings. Hope is positive beliefs combined with action toward a clear goal.

At times you may need to let go of hope for your psychological well-being. Relinquishing hope that your abusive partner will change even after you have put forth your best efforts in the relationship is dangerous. Likewise, you can't hope to win the golf tournament when you are nine strokes behind the leader on the last hole. Abandoning hope is hard because you must accept that you were unsuccessful this time and experience the plethora of emotions that comes with that. Fortunately, surrendering hope when it is prudent permits you to redirect your attention and efforts elsewhere to achieve a modified or improved goal.

Two decades of scientific research by Martin Seligman suggests that hope enhances happiness, improves your quality of life, relieves stress, and reduces feelings of helplessness.[165] Simply put, hope makes life better.

Mental toughness is the ability to resist, handle, and conquer doubts, worries, and circumstances that prevent you from completing an objective. It encompasses a winner's mindset, vigilance, grit, perseverance, and character. It is a term widely used in athletics and can be the difference between winning and losing, especially when talents, skills, and physical abilities are comparable. Research concluded that hope is directly correlated with an athlete's mental toughness.[166] Mental toughness is important for nonathletes as well. It enables you to persevere through adversity long enough to relish your triumphant victory.

Our major defense against despair, anxiety, distress, depression, or burnout is hope. Without it, we are caught in the moment and don't see ourselves overcoming these feelings in the future. People with kidney failure experience high levels of distress, anxiety, depression, and despair as they endure dialysis and await a lifesaving kidney transplant. A clinical trial assessed the benefits of hope therapy versus nonspecific intervention in individuals undergoing hemodialysis.[167] Participants joined in hope therapy for 60 to 90 minutes during dialysis once per week for a total of eight sessions. Remarkably, the hope therapy group experienced reduced depression, anxiety, and stress before, immediately following, and for one month after the intervention. On the contrary, the nonspecific intervention group experienced no benefits at all. Hope is the foundation that drives people with addictions to find a better way and heal. Hope therapy reduced depression, increased hopefulness, and improved recovery in people with addictions.[168,169] Other research found that having hope is a major key in recovering from anxiety disorders.[170] Hope promotes emotional resilience and balance in life, even when faced with very challenging circumstances.

Hopeful people maintain longer, more satisfying relationships as well. Let's face it: no one likes to be around someone who's a constant pessimist. Eventually, that cynical outlook on life rubs off on you. A study of 108 couples who had been dating for at least six months reported that people in relationships with at least one optimist had greater relationship satisfaction.[171] These couples perceived greater support in the relationship, felt more investment in the relationship, and resolved conflict more effectively. After one year, the researchers observed that people in relationships with at least one optimist were more likely to remain together. The good news from this research is that only one of the people in the relationship needs to be an optimist for it to be more fulfilling and longer-lasting.

School is tough at every level. You are trying to fit in, learn, and achieve academic success simultaneously. If you're going to college, you may also be facing financial stress to pay for your education. Hope is imperative to academic success. Research shows that students with high levels of optimism are more likely to have high-quality friendships, be more engaged in their studies, possess greater resilience, and get better grades.[172,173,174,175] Being hopeful is important for students at every level of education.

A sense of hope may even promote a longer, healthier life. Researchers exploring the implications of hope for health and well-being found that older adults with a greater sense of hope had better physical and psychological well-being.[176] Hopeful older adults had a lower risk of dying from all causes, fewer chronic health conditions, a lower risk of cancer, and fewer sleep problems. In addition, they had greater life satisfaction, lower distress, improved social well-being, and a greater sense of life purpose. Another study tracked more than 71,000 men and women for ten to thirty years—69,744 women for ten years and 1,429 men for thirty years—to determine if hope prolongs life.[177] Men and women with the highest levels of hope and optimism lived, on average, 11 to 15 percent longer, and were significantly more likely to reach the age of 85 when compared to the least optimistic people. This emerging research suggests that hopeful people live longer, healthier lives with fewer chronic health conditions.

Your emotional response to pain can either diminish or amplify the pain you are feeling. Hope can be a coping mechanism for chronic pain because it makes you feel better as you anticipate relief in the future. Researchers in Spain compared how being on the upper end of the hope spectrum (optimism) compared to being on the lower end of the hope spectrum (pessimism) affected ninety-eight people with chronic pain.[178] Optimistic individuals were more likely to engage in active coping strategies that reduced pain, anxiety, depression, and impairment, and promoted high levels of functioning in life. Quite the reverse, pessimists relied on passive coping—removes personal responsibility for managing the stressor and relies on external sources—and experienced higher levels of pain, anxiety, depression, and impairment and low levels of functioning. A review article also concluded that hope is a useful intervention for not only chronic pain, but many chronic illnesses.[179] Hope is an important therapeutic factor for any illness because it causes adaptations in the brain that change the way we respond to illness, injury, and pain.

Remarkably, hopefulness has even been associated with better immune function. Specifically, researchers found that optimism increased the number of helper T cells (CD4+) and natural killer cell (NKC) cytotoxicity.[180] Helper T cells are a type of immune cell that plays a central role in normal immune responses by releasing chemicals that activate other immune cells. These cells help the immune system recognize and respond to foreign substances. NKCs are also immune cells that control several types of cancerous cells and infections caused by pathogens. They possess the ability to kill cancerous and pathogenic cells, limiting their spread and the subsequent damage they cause. Feeling more hopeful about the future, in this case, may also help you feel better literally, or at least stay healthier.

The Plymouth Pilgrims understood that hope is not contingent on circumstances. They learned the profound truth that hope brings peace and joy. Seeking religious freedom, a congregation of hopeful English Protestants left their homes in Scrooby, Nottinghamshire, England, in 1608. These "separatists" refused to pledge allegiance to the corrupt and idolatrous Church of England and hoped for freedom to worship as their consciences dictated in Holland.

Indeed, these Saints, as they called themselves, found religious freedom in Holland, but also found secular life more difficult to navigate. Dutch craft guilds practiced exclusionary methods that prevented migrants from earning a living wage. Instead, they were consigned to tedious, unskilled, and low-paying jobs. More alarming to the group was the fact that Holland provided an environment for their children to be enticed away by evil. For this devout group, it meant they must put their faith and hope in finding a new home once again.

After returning to England, the Saints prepared for a journey to the New World across the Atlantic Ocean. They received permission from the King of England to leave the Church of England "provided they carried themselves peaceably." They received permission from the Virginia Company to establish a settlement on the East Coast between 38 and 41 degrees north latitude. And they coordinated for passage on two merchant ships—the *Mayflower* and the *Speedwell*. Exercising faith and hope, they boarded the two ships in August of 1620. However, the *Speedwell* began to leak almost immediately, forcing them to return to port at Plymouth.

After consolidating their belongings and themselves to the *Mayflower*, they set sail again. The delays in departure forced them to cross the Atlantic during the height of the storm season, making the journey very unpleasant. Following two miserable months at sea, the Saints arrived in the New World. They quickly discovered that they had arrived in the wrong place—Cape Cod, which is located outside their area of permission to colonize at 42 degrees north latitude.

Maintaining hope and optimism, the Saints drafted and signed the Mayflower Compact to establish a civil society. This document swore allegiance to the English king, but also paved the way for self-government by elected officials and just and equal laws. Their hope for something better motivated them to endure an arduous journey to the New World.

If you lack hope in your life, don't fret—it can be increased gradually.

Find a clear direction. If you were going hiking in unfamiliar territory, you'd probably rely on a map, maybe a compass as well, to navigate your way to the end. Being able to see the path you need to follow and the steps you need to take to make it to your desired destination is essential to having hope. Write down your plan in detailed, but small and manageable, steps outlining how you will get to your end goal. With a clear direction to achieve the objective, you are more likely to realize victory and success.

Leverage past wins. Looking back at times you set a goal, hoped to achieve it, and realized that a goal can increase your happiness and hope for the future.[181] Set a regular time—weekly, monthly, and yearly—to review your goal progress and celebrate wins.

Pray or meditate. One of the most common ways people find hope is to pray, and research supports this practice. Interestingly, investigation suggests that the type of prayer is important. In a study of 430 people, those who participated in three forms of prayer (adoration—solely focused on worship of God; thanksgiving—expressing thanks for blessings; and reception—seeking divine guidance or understanding) experienced improved psychological well-being.[182] Conversely, prayers of confession, supplication—asking for help in specific life events, or obligatory prayers had a negative effect or no effect at all. You don't need to be religious to pray. God loves and listens to each of His children. If you prefer not to pray, meditate. Meditation focuses your mind and trains your attention leading to a calmer state. With greater awareness, you will be able to find greater hope.

Filter negative news. It's important to be aware of local and world events, but sometimes the barrage of negative news is depressing. Exposure to constant negative news can shape your worldview in a destructive way, particularly if you are struggling yourself. Take a break from the news, including social media, and seek out some inspiring media or comedy to lighten the load on your shoulders.

Maintain a growth mindset. If you lose hope, your mind tends to fixate on negativity and believe that the worst things will happen. A growth mindset instills a robust belief that you can grow through hard work and perseverance. Frame failures as temporary setbacks that you can learn from. This reveals ways you can improve and conveys hope for the future. Indeed, failure teaches you things you cannot learn from success.

Identify and strive to refrain from negative thoughts. Recognizing negative thought patterns is a vital step to hope. When you find them creeping into your mind, seek to refocus them to a hopeful thought instead. Consider the ABCDE model of cognitive behavioral therapy. A is for adversity, where you identify the problem. B is for belief and involves evaluating the negative belief you have about the challenge. C examines the consequences that belief is having on your emotions and behavior. D means you dispute those beliefs and mindfully examine, question, and challenge them. The last step, E, is when you notice their effects and propose alternate explanations to yourself that are more reasonable and plausible.

Give hope to others. Spreading hope to others inherently brings hope to your life. Our brains are wired to derive pleasure when we give hope to others. This happens because dopamine and oxytocin—happy hormones connected to the reward and pleasure centers of our brain—are activated when we serve others. Passing on hope to others triggers our brain's pleasure centers sufficiently to produce feelings as strong as if we received hope ourselves.

We must build enduring hope that our actions will have a ripple effect to change the world. We are not helplessly controlled by the ruling elite. Ultimately, we control our destinies. We outnumber them by a significant margin and only allow them to maintain control because of ignorance and apathy. We must not remain passive and instead actively seek escape by first having the hope that we can change the current situation.

> Happiness can be found, even in the darkest of
> times, if one only remembers to turn on the light.
>
> —Albus Dumbledore in *Harry Potter and
> the Prisoner of Azkaban* by J. K. Rowling

CHAPTER 13

COURAGE

The opposite for courage is not cowardice, it is conformity. Even a dead fish can go with the flow.

—Jim Hightower

It is difficult, if not impossible, to cultivate the other traits without courage. Courage encapsulates the entirety of life. We must be brave to be kind, inclusive, respectful, positive, compassionate, empathetic, loving, persistent, and so forth. Frankly, it takes courage to do just about anything in life. Courage is a mental, emotional, physical, or spiritual preparedness and capacity to deal with difficult circumstances. Courage is important to overcome the elite's control not just because it takes courage to oppose them, but because it takes great courage to recognize faults in our own thinking and actions and correct them.

Books, fairy tales, and movies are replete with inspirational stories of courageous heroes. These stories often portray bravery in the face of great physical threat, but courage is much more than physical bravery. It is speaking out against injustice, taking risks to achieve your dreams, having courage to speak in front of a large audience despite stifling anxiety, asking your crush on a date, engaging in a new experience, asking for a raise at work, and far more. Life is full of risks, big and small. Courage is taking action even though the outcome is unclear.

Not a day goes by that you don't exercise courage. You need courage to begin something in spite of uncertainty. Stephen King said, "The scariest moment is always just before you start. After that, things can only get better." Anticipatory fear can prevent us from exercising courage. Ambiguity creates doubt, and doubt fear. We primarily experience two types of fear: fear that detects physical danger and fear of damaging our ego. When fear arises from something outside a physical threat, it not just psychological in nature, but ego-driven fear. Fear of failure, loss, being alone, rejection, physical harm, or looking foolish, all challenge courage.

Moral courage is the courage to take action to enforce societal and ethical norms despite the risk of adverse consequences. Moral cowardice, on the contrary, involves dodging action when faced with moral or ethical challenges because of selfishness and fear. Modern society, as a whole, lacks moral courage. Politicians take positions contrary to their personal core beliefs to place party over their constituents and maintain a position of authority. People stay in jobs where they commit unethical acts daily for fear of lack of resources. Others remain quiet when they are material witnesses to a crime because they fear retribution. No matter the reason, moral cowardice eats at your conscious and cankers the soul.

An escaped slave, nurse, and Union spy, Harriet Tubman became the "conductor" of the Underground Railroad that freed approximately seventy enslaved individuals—and reportedly instructed dozens of others how to escape—despite great risk to herself. She completed thirteen rescue missions all while facing a bounty for her capture. Her desire for justice was apparent at age twelve when she stepped between a slaveowner who was preparing to throw a heavy weight at a fugitive. The weight hit her in the head causing a deep wound and traumatic brain injury. Tubman didn't think of only herself after escaping slavery; she desired this same freedom she had realized for all enslaved people. Her moral convictions propelled her to act on behalf of

158

others. She is an icon of American history who exhibited tremendous moral courage.

Abraham Lincoln has inspired generations with his courage, character, and perseverance. As an Illinois state legislator, Lincoln engaged in a series of antislavery measures at a time when it took great courage to speak or write against slavery. His constituents in Illinois largely consisted of emigrants from slave states with deeply engrained prejudices who were prone to violence against people who expressed antislavery sentiments. Notwithstanding these circumstances, he composed a solemn protest against cruel laws enacted against people of color called "the Black Code." As the sixteenth president of the United States, his antislavery actions were consummated in the Emancipation Proclamation and the Constitutional Amendment that abolished slavery forever in the United States. For many, he represents standing for what is right in the face of great opposition.

Although largely unknown, Alice Paul's courage ignited a powerful force that won women the right to vote in the United States. Her mother got Alice involved in women's suffrage (the movement to grant women the right to vote) by taking her to suffrage meetings as a young girl. Her desire for equal rights for women was sustained as she grew older. After graduating college, she moved to Washington and organized protests, demonstrations, and parades pursuing equal rights for women. Her protesting landed her in jail several times, where she was beaten, handcuffed in her cell, and forced to live in very poor conditions. Undeterred by this, she staged a hunger strike. For her troubles, she was placed in a straitjacket and force-fed raw eggs until she vomited. Prison officials even attempted to have a psychiatrist declare her insane. Bravely, the psychiatrist declared that "courage in women is often mistaken for insanity." Paul upheld her conviction in the face of great adversity, and eventually, her courage prompted changes in attitudes toward women's suffrage at the highest office in the land—President Woodrow Wilson. Her courage to stand up for all women led to the long-overdue right of women to vote.

Fostering courage when your hands are shaking and your heart is pounding out of your chest is challenging, to say the least. It is even more difficult to muster courage when faced with threat of incarceration or physical harm. Yet those who exercise courage and endure hardships often reap substantial reward for themselves and others.

Build courage slowly. Courage doesn't appear overnight, and it takes time to gradually expand your comfort zone. For instance, if you have a fear of public speaking don't make your first speech in front of a stadium thirty thousand people strong. Instead, start with a small group of a few people and gradually increase your audience size as you feel more confident and comfortable.

Modify your perspective. It is human nature to be harsher on yourself than you are on others. Knowing this, fear of harming ego will be enlarged when we consider potential nonphysical harm to ourselves. The next time you are stretching your comfort zone, change your perspective. Ask yourself how you would perceive your friend in the same situation. Doing so can reframe the self-talk we are engaged in that contributes to psychological fear. Recognize your negative biases that cause you to pay more attention to disapproval than positive feedback. Detractors are usually in the minority, despite what our negative self-talk tells us, so actively notice positive reinforcement.

Show courage for issues you are passionate about. It's easier to be courageous if we are passionate about the issue or situation. For instance, if your ten-year-old son's school is on a busy street, you will likely be more passionate about measures involving his safety walking home than you would about whether he should learn cursive or not. You will therefore have more courage to talk to the principal and the city about ways to make walking to and from school safer.

Find courage in numbers. It's much easier to act when you have the strength of numbers. One of the hardest things to do is to stand alone on an issue, and oftentimes there are issues worth standing alone for. However, gathering more people to your cause makes being courageous easier.

Acknowledge existing courage. Recognize places that you already possess courage. You may fear public speaking but frequently exhibit courage by trying new things. Everyone possesses courage, no matter how simple or nonvisible. Recognizing even a smidgen of your courage will help you know that you own the trait and can further develop it.

Avoid comparisons. Each of us is unique, with distinctive skills, talents, and abilities. It does not help to compare yourself to others. Some people will possess courage in areas you don't, and you possess courage in ways they don't. You should focus on comparing yourself only against your past self. Have you improved from yesterday, a week, or a month ago? Focusing on your improvement is critical to building greater confidence.

Take risks and accept failure. You must take risks to build courage. You'll fail to build courage if you cower in your easy chair at home and never leave the house. Sometimes you will "fail," and that is OK. Accept that temporary failure is a fact of life and no one escapes it. Embrace failure as part of your courage-building process. The important thing is that you keep moving forward and take calculated risks.

There is a global pandemic occurring right now, and it is the absence of courage. It stems from a desire to avoid accepting personal responsibility, not honoring our values, and seeing ourselves as victims. We need more courageous individuals today, people who are willing to make courageous decisions and face the outcomes head-on. Moral courage takes honesty and immovable integrity, including being honest with ourselves. Charles Marshall once said, "Integrity is doing the right thing, even when no one is looking." It takes courage to do what is right at all times and in all places. We may think that no one will notice if we cheat on a test or steal from a store, but we know and must live with those actions. "Courage is the first of human qualities because it is the quality that guarantees all the others," Winston Churchill rightly said. Courage is a vital skill and character trait that is absolutely required to improve world societies. It takes courage to be true to yourself, to be you, and to rise above the fears prostituted by the ruling elites.

> Courage isn't having the strength to go on—it is going on when you don't have strength.
>
> —Napoleon Bonaparte

CHAPTER 14

PATIENCE

A man who is a master of patience is master
of everything else.

—George Savile

While patience is a virtue, it is also a life skill that requires constant refining. As a state of being between experience and reaction, patience is needed for yourself, others, and life in general. It involves awareness and management of your thoughts and emotions in relation to the experience. Cultivating patience in your life leads to less stress, anger, anxiety, and frustration. Patience makes us better humans.

Isn't it interesting that having patience, not finding a solution, is among the most common advice given to a person when facing adversity? Practicing patience allows us to reduce worry when things don't go as planned or take longer than we want. Momentous life events like waiting for your dream job, recovering from a car accident, waiting for test results from your doctor, and awaiting the arrival of your baby test your patience. Even the little things in life require patience. How often have you gotten irritated because the line in the grocery store is not moving fast enough, your computer took too long to reboot, or you were stuck in traffic? Dream achievement requires the ability to overcome challenges and obstacles, and this is very challenging, if not impossible, to do without patience.

Like courage, patience is directly linked to many of the other attributes we've already covered. Patience helps you develop empathy. Taking the time to understand the motives behind a person's actions allows you to truly see them and have more compassion for why they may act the way they do. An infant's cry can be irritating, particularly if it is prolonged. Yet the infant has no other means of communicating that she is hungry, needs a diaper changed, or any of her other many needs, except crying. Charity is also connected to patience. When we are not easily provoked and willing to bear all things, we are more charitable to others.[183] Patience helps us accept other people as they are.

Positivity requires patience. In today's society of instant gratification, few people have the patience to wait for good things to happen. We are easily frustrated when things don't go the way we want them. However, no amount of whining and stomping your feet will make a good thing happen faster. Most of us learned this as toddlers unless our parents enabled this behavior by rewarding it. Great things take time and don't happen at the snap of a finger. When the unexpected happens, reframe the situation, look for the positive, and exercise patience.

Intelligent and rational thought is quickly derailed by impatience. People make impulsive and reckless decisions when they lack patience. Impatience also breeds anger, which drives away our conscience and shuts down our cognitive capabilities. Applying patience increases our capacity to think clearly and arrive at intelligent, logical, and reasonable conclusions.

Impatience clouds our reasoning and makes us irritable. In this state of mind, we may say or do things that hurt the people we love, our friends, or relationships with neighbors, coworkers, associates, and even strangers. Most of us can relate to focusing on something on our smartphone—a work email or even a trivial video—only to be interrupted by a young child who wants our attention. Our immediate reaction is to be upset and irritable, maybe even scold the child. Don't think you respond this way? Observe your initial emotions and thoughts the next time you are interrupted while devoting time to the screen on your phone, computer, or tablet. However, those who have learned the virtue of patience will hold those thoughts and actions and respond in a calm and kind way. Consequently, if you care about your relationships, you need to cultivate patience and be mindful of the other person's qualities, motives, and challenges before speaking and acting.

Apparently, we can learn a lot from a marshmallow and a child. In the 1970s, Stanford researchers conducted an experiment to test a child's patience with the ultimate goal to see if patience as a child translated to greater success later in life.[184] Preschool-age children had a single treat (a marshmallow or pretzel stick depending on the child's preference) placed in front of them and were told that if they waited for a period of time, they would receive two treats. Researchers left the child alone in the room for about fifteen minutes and then returned. The opportunity for the child was to double their reward. Some children didn't have the patience to wait for a double reward and ate their treat during the fifteen minutes. Other children exercised a great deal of patience and chose not to eat the treat. During follow-up studies decades later, the researchers found that children who exercise patience tended to perform better in life—such as better academic performance and improved health.[185,186,187,188]

In 2018, the original study was replicated and extended (over nine hundred children instead of the original ninety), with a group of children more representative of the general population.[189] They also controlled for socioeconomic factors. What the researchers observed was that socioeconomic background was more predictive of success later in life than patience. Children from wealthier homes exercised greater patience, whereas children in households with fewer means tended to eat the marshmallow quickly. However, one could argue that the background of the children significantly shaped their level of patience. Kids from poor homes might be less motivated to wait for a second marshmallow because daily life holds fewer guarantees and they have lived in a home where food in the pantry today does not guarantee it will be there tomorrow. On the contrary, children from affluent homes are used to adequate resources and therefore more able to delay gratification. This later experiment suggests that patience is a product of our environment.

Job provides a classic example of patience in the Bible. After losing most of his worldly possessions, including his children, he experienced the physical challenge of boils. This wasn't the end of his suffering, though. His friends lacked empathy for and turned on him. Despite facing substantial challenges and trials, Job remained faithful and patient. His patience wasn't perfect, nor should we expect ours to be, but he did persevere. Because of his patience in suffering, Job was blessed with greater prosperity in the latter part of his life than what he had been blessed with in the beginning.

Cultivating an attitude of patience is no easy task; it takes arduous practice. With time and effort, you will find that you are more patient with yourself and others.

Be mindful of your impatience. The first step to developing patience is to identify what people, events, and circumstances tend to set you off. Be aware of the signs that you are becoming impatient, such as increased agitation, discomfort, and even an uncomfortable feeling in your stomach. During these early moments of impatience, be mindful of and manage your thoughts and reactions. Initial thoughts and reactions are often clouded by the discomfort of impatience.

Take a deep breath. Deep breathing slows down and resets your nervous system to increase parasympathetic activity.[190] Increased parasympathetic activity places you in a condition of healing and balanced nervous system function. Take ten deep breaths when are faced with a challenge to your patience to help you center. After taking these deep breaths, chances are you will be in a calmer state that will allow you to respond rationally and with greater patience.

Relax your muscles. Impatience can initiate your fight-or-flight response, which causes your muscles to tense up. Consciously focus on relaxing your muscles by tightening them individually and then releasing them (e.g., calves, then biceps, and so on). This physical release of muscle tension may trigger your mind to release the psychological tension as well.

Laugh often. Sometimes the best way to handle a difficult situation is to laugh. Laughing appropriately—for example, we wouldn't laugh maniacally at a somber funeral—releases feel-good endorphins that are helpful when you are uncomfortable or sad.[191] Laughter can create connections between people, even when in tense situations because it resets your mind and body. Master the art of laughter with good intentions to foster patience.

Be empathetic. Empathy is especially important if your impatience is triggered by a person. Practicing empathy when you realize you are impatient acknowledges the feelings and emotions of the other person. See them deeply and seek to understand what they are going through at that moment. Doing so, helps you experience the situation from their vantage point and encourages you to question whether impatience is an appropriate response to that situation.

Challenge your perception. Your intrinsic motivations and life experiences shape your perception of your situations. Another person will likely perceive things differently because they too are shaped by personal motivations and experiences. See the situation through the lens of the other person when possible. If there's time, seek perspective from a trusted individual. They may be able to help you reconcile the varying perspectives in the situation. Ask

167

yourself if your perception is the Truth or only your truth. If it is only your truth, embrace a new perspective.

Embrace discomfort. Being patient is not always comfortable, and it is unpleasant to pursue a path outside what feels natural. Building patience forces you to be uncomfortable, but with practice, this discomfort will slowly fade, and patience will feel like a natural state.

Patience brings peace to your life and kindles a desire to accept other people for who they are, flaws and all. Negative emotions like frustration and anger happen and patience is the antidote, bringing immense emotional freedom. Patience will be required as we connect with those who we are taught to oppose, and participate in uncomfortable conversations. You have a choice in how you respond to challenges. Staying calm and centered by practicing patience will improve all areas of your life.

> Patience is to be calm no matter what happens, constantly take action to turn it to positive growth opportunities, and have faith to believe that it will all work out in the end while you are waiting.
>
> —Roy T. Bennett

CHAPTER 15

THE BOLD PATH FORWARD

Freedom makes a huge requirement of every human being. With freedom comes responsibility. For the person who is unwilling to grow up, the person who does not want to carry his own weight, this is a frightening prospect.

—Eleanor Roosevelt

We have a responsibility to use the divine intelligence each one of us possesses. Don't just obey orders; think for yourselves. We can no longer boast the ability to see, hear, and think, but live life as though we were blind, deaf, and unable to reason. Misinformation and deception easily sway those who fail to accurately see, hear, and think. The ruling elite pursues strategies that erode humanity into subservient sleepwalkers. How long will it take for the masses to snap out of it and wake up from the engineered social conditioning?

The ruling elite's control of the world is fragile and reliant upon a submissive and apathetic public. This group that includes the very wealthy, journalists, faculty and administration at prestigious universities, opportunistic entrepreneurs, government agency employees, bioengineers, coders, bankers, judges, and lawyers controls global economies and the flow of information. Hiding behind a massive charade greater than Oz himself could invent, the elites impose themselves on virtually everything for the sole purpose of gain. They want more ownership, unchecked power, windfall profits, and political dominance. Leveraging our desire to support social causes we feel passionate about, they flaunt tolerance, outcome equality, environmentalism, or whatever other ethos they can fabricate to get people to do things "for the greater good," which really means for the good of the elite. *New York Times* contributor Tim Kreider said, "Outrage is like a lot of other things that feel good but over time devour us from the inside out. And it's even more insidious than most vices because we don't even consciously acknowledge that it's a pleasure." For the greater good sounds promising, but it is actually the elite's way of rationalizing their behavior while using other people as mere means to their own insidious ends.

It's cliché, but question everything. Simply accepting an implanted narrative, even if most people do so without questioning, represents tolerance for a deceptive reality. Question the motives of media, politicians, government employees and entities, massive corporations, the education system, and everything else. We must discover the actual motives of any person or organization that imposes restrictions on freedoms. Break free from the imprisoning mental, emotional, physical, and spiritual chains inflicted on you by the ruling elite and their coconspirators. Stop being complicit in their controlling activities. Live an authentic life with freedom and purpose.

Virtue signaling is used as a tool to recruit common folk in the solicitation of others to do the elite's bidding. Virtue signaling is a term used to describe people who perform empty acts showing support for a social cause without actually doing anything meaningful to advance it. The response to COVID-19 has been a perfect example of this practice and indeed amplified its performance. Entertainers and politicians virtue signal wearing masks, staying home, and social distancing, while they host lavish awards shows and parties, entertain wealthy donors at restaurants, and generally refuse to obey the restrictions they themselves extol and implement. Celebrities, politicians, and others are all too

170

willing to share their condescending virtue signaling to the ordinary people from their safe and comfortable mansions. These attention-seeking individuals use virtue signaling as the perfect opportunity to display just how important and irreplaceable they think they are.

In response to COVID-19, the public was told to sacrifice two weeks of freedom to preserve long-term prosperity and health. Lockdowns and restrictions implemented on freedoms by overzealous, power-hungry governors and other people in authority around the world were willingly accepted as responsible measures to fight a respiratory illness. Said Sam Houston, "When tyrants ask you to yield one jot of your liberty, and you consent thereto, it is the first link forged in the chain that will eventually hold you in bondage." More than a year later, many have not relented on their restrictions. They refuse to acknowledge the evidence that lockdowns and restrictions have done more harm than good. Indeed, a team of Stanford researchers found that they had a minimal impact of slowing the spread of COVID-19.[192] The study compared the harsh lockdown policies (business closures and stay-at-home orders) of eight countries: England, France, Germany, Iran, Italy, Netherlands, Spain, and the United States versus light-lockdown policies (contact tracing, large gathering restrictions, targeted quarantines, and the use of general guidance) implemented in South Korea and Sweden. In other words, countries that shut down society contrasted to those who caused minor inconveniences instead. The conclusion was that the unprecedented harsh restrictions provided little benefit over lighter and less intrusive limitations.

Other research reveals that the harms of harsh lockdown policies are ten times greater than any perceived benefit.[193] Alarmists initially and falsely perpetuated an infection fatality rate of 2–3 percent and projected that 80 percent of the world's population would be infected. This doomsday misinformation was repeatedly shared to justify harsh lockdowns, but accurate and factual data proved that the median infection fatality rate was 0.23 percent, and this dropped to 0.05 percent if you are under seventy years old. Similarly, COVID-19 alarmists are already preparing the population mentally for further restrictions on freedom by warning of a second or third wave of the virus. While more than 2.6 million deaths have been attributed to COVID-19—which are undoubtedly inflated, the study estimates that millions more people globally have been adversely affected by the unnecessary practice of lockdowns.

Adverse outcomes cited in the study include the following:

- Food insecurity increased 82 percent, placing 82–132 million more people in a hunger crisis.
- Extreme poverty increased by an estimated seventy million people.
- Increased deaths from other infectious diseases (tuberculosis, malaria, HIV) from interrupted medical services may cause hundreds of thousands, perhaps more than a million, extra deaths in the next year.
- Maternal and child (under age five) mortality increased by 1.7 million because of interrupted health care.
- Earning potential decreased because of school closures, which also crippled children's education.
- Domestic violence intensified for millions of women (20 percent increase).
- Suicides increased—Japan experienced more suicide deaths than deaths from COVID in October of 2020.[194]
- Abortions became more unsafe (2.7 million additional) because of disrupted access to contraceptives.
- Years of life were lost because of poorer mental health: United States 67.58 million, Canada 7.79 million, United Kingdom 13.62 million.

While the working class suffered from the unwarranted harsh lockdown policies, the wealthy elites profited. According to a report by Swiss bank UBS, billionaires increased their wealth to a record-high \$10.2 trillion during COVID restrictions (by October 2020).[195] To put this in perspective, the previous peak wealth achieved by moneyed elites was \$8.9 trillion in 2017. The superrich weren't harmed by the pandemic; they directly benefited from it. Their plan to capture wealth worked flawlessly.

Another report from December 2020 found that ten of the wealthiest individuals in the world alone boosted their wealth an astonishing \$400 billion during COVID.[196] Among them, Jeff Bezos (Amazon), Elon Musk (Tesla), Bernard Arnault (LVMH), Mark Zuckerberg (Facebook), Larry Page (Google), and Bill Gates (Bill and Melinda Gates Foundation) each profited considerably as world poverty dramatically increased. Of all tyrannies, tyranny performed under the guise of the good of its victims may be the most oppressive. The poor became poorer, and the rich became richer "for the greater good."

The mishandling of COVID, including suppression of dissenting opinions and rushed experimental shots, calls to mind multiple tragic and unethical experiments performed on humans. Indeed, the moneyed elites and government agencies that support them have the potential to profit billions of dollars from experimental shots that also make them seem as if they are seeking the best interests of society. Moneyed elites can be called philanthropists, as they throw their money behind seemingly helpful causes that actually benefit the elites.

One of the most notorious human trials in recent history is the unethical and terrible Tuskegee experiment perpetrated on the black community from 1932 to 1972. Under the facade of free medical care for "bad blood," the US Public Health Service (USPHS) recruited six hundred black men for a project that was actually intended to observe the natural course of untreated syphilis infections. The experiment included 399 men with latent syphilis and a control group of 201 men without the disease.

Researchers intentionally withheld effective medical interventions—including penicillin, which became the recommended treatment for syphilis halfway through the experiment in 1947—to track the infection's full progression. The goal was to autopsy each man in the experiment after he died.

During the mid-1960s, a USPHS venereal disease investigator named Peter Buxton found out about the Tuskegee experiment and expressed concerns about the ethics of the trial. In response, the USPHS formed a committee to evaluate his concerns but ultimately rejected them and chose to continue the experiment. In other words, discovery was more important than humanity. Unsatisfied with the panel's decision, Buxton leaked the story to a reporter and eventually another reporter broke the story in July 1972, prompting significant public outrage and forcing the experiment to end.

By the end of the experiment, 128 participants had died directly from syphilis or its complications, at least forty spouses contracted syphilis, and nineteen of the participant's children had been born with the infection. Tuskegee instilled a lingering mistrust of the medical system among the black community that persists today. This horrific experiment lacked humanity and made unsuspecting participants human Guinea pigs. It represents yet another atrocious act committed by government officials in the name of good for all of society.

A mistrust in government-sponsored medical care is justified given the sordid history of government agencies and their untried medical interventions. The black community are not the only victims of immoral experiments aimed at discovering curative remedies to profit from. Extremely disgraceful experiments were also performed on mentally handicapped children from Willowbrook State School located in Staten Island, New York, from 1956 to 1970. Children were intentionally infected with hepatitis in an attempt to track the effects of various experimental drugs on the illness.[197] Many of the children died during the experiments. Unethical scientists justified their actions by claiming that the children were in an environment where hepatitis was prevalent, so they were bound to get it anyway. However, their actions amounted to preying on the vulnerable to satisfy their own awful desires.

Vulnerable, easy to control, and often unsuspecting victims seem to be the government's preferential target for immoral experiments. Control is a central principle of any experiment, and both the elites and the government agencies that serve them know this. The US government conducted a malaria experiment during the 1940s in the Stateville Penitentiary (Crest Hill, Illinois, United States).[198] Over 400 inmates were illegally infected with malaria in a misguided effort to find a cure for the disease. Interestingly, the government got the prisoners to do their dirty work on this one. Tests were administered and documented exclusively by the prisoners themselves and the prisoners even selected who was included in the experiment. Unfortunately, the experimental drugs administered frequently had irreversible and vicious side effects, such as severe toxicity and heart failure. Even though the experiment was immoral, it was praised for the potential benefits it provided to society and seen as a necessary sacrifice required of the prisoners to pay back their debts to society.

Using captive populations means big money for medical researchers. From 1955 to 1960, Sonoma State Hospital in northern California served as a permanent housing center for children born with disorders such as cerebral palsy. Infirm children were subjected to various experiments including exposure to radiation and spinal taps just to observe the effects.[199] There was no real benefit to the tests that were performed without any parental consent. Most records of these experiments have been destroyed, but one report claims that over 1,400 people died at the clinic.[200] Unconscionably, a hospital designated for the care of the infirm became a mad scientists' lab with disturbed researchers performing unethical experiments on the defenseless.

From 1989 to 1991, the US Centers for Disease Control and Prevention conducted experiments involving the measles vaccine.[201] To find out if a high-potency Edmonston-Zagreb measles vaccine could be safely administered to infants as young as four months old, researchers injected thousands of babies in Third World countries (African nations and Haiti). Despite multiple immune side effects and deaths among these infants, the government continued their trials in more than 1,500 black and Hispanic infants in Los Angeles, California. The CDC later admitted that they did not inform the parents that their children were being injected with an experimental vaccine with known risks. The corrupt experiment only ended when it came to light in America that children in Africa and Haiti died at an alarming rate within two years of receiving the more potent dosage of the vaccine being investigated.

These are just a few of the examples demonstrating that unscrupulous individuals are willing to commit untold barbarities in the name of discovery and ultimately profit. Elites and their coconspirators pursue discovery of medicines that bring windfall profits at the expense of their neighbors and fellow citizens. More than a century ago, Oscar Wilde wrote, "Just as the worst slave-owners were those who were kind to their slaves, and so prevented the horror of the system being realised by those who suffered from it, and understood by those who contemplated it, so, in the present state of things . . . the people who do most harm are the people who try to do most good." Currently, that harm is the concentration of wealth among the moneyed elites and a virtual monopoly on the benefits of change. A pattern of misinformation, lack of transparency, and inhumane experimentation has been established, which is still playing out today among unwitting participants.

Today, people who believe in a reality outside the official narrative perpetuated by the elites are called conspiracy theorists or spreaders of dangerous misinformation. This tactic diminishes the credibility of the individual and the validity of what they say, and discourages others from believing them. Free speech is taken away to limit their influence. Those in control don't want more people realizing they have accepted and are living in a bogus reality. Censorship is a giant step toward the toppling of freedom. Benjamin Franklin declared, "Whoever would overthrow the liberty of a nation must begin by subduing the freeness of speech." Freedom involves personal responsibility. As a consequence, many people chose safety and security because they fear the responsibility of freedom.

Continuing the COVID response as our example, when a panel of healthcare professionals from Harvard, Stanford, and Oxford offered a different perspective on the nation's COVID response, the media chose to ignore or vilify them. Among other things, the panelists agreed that lockdowns were ineffective—perhaps the single biggest mistake in medical history, contract tracing was a failure, mask mandates caused more harm than good, and schools should be opened. These brave doctors exposed the negative impacts of the media during COVID. Specifically, they revealed that the media spread fear and silenced dissenting opinions that poked holes in the MSM's preferred narrative that lockdowns were vital, contract tracing important, masks the end-all for protection, and open schools were a public threat. In retaliation to the panel put together by Florida governor Ron DeSantis, the media sought to label the distinguished and credentialed panelists as "controversial," "outside the mainstream," or "dangerous." In other words, they should not be trusted, and you should only listen to the media, who have no medical training whatsoever. How was the information the panel shared dangerous? It wasn't dangerous to the public. It was dangerous to the media narrative critical to controlling the populace.

In the 1900s, Italian civil engineer, sociologist, economist, political scientist, and philosopher Vilfredo Pareto wrote a magnum opus called *Trattato Di Sociologia Generale* (*Treatise on General Sociology*), wherein he argued that the elites always rule.[202] He identified two types of elite rulers he called foxes and lions. Foxes dominate as part of a shadow game through manipulation, deceit, cunning, and cooptation (taking over or appropriating something for a different purpose). Lions are more visible, ruling through established hierarchical bureaucracies and force if necessary. Pareto taught that the pendulum of rule swings from one type of elite to the other—foxes to lions and back again.

Meaningful change to regain humanity takes time and effort. More of us will need to work toward restoring and maintaining power and freedom with the people than are working against it. We need more aware individuals operating outside the slave consciousness. Hijacking the planet requires controlling the population without them even knowing it. Once a person becomes aware, the ability to control them like a puppet becomes far more challenging. A minority of us recognize what is happening, but the majority are still among the sleeping masses complying with the elite's bidding. People need to recognize that many of their own thoughts and beliefs are programmed and implanted to serve the elites and dehumanize society. A willingness to deny reality and accept false narratives pervades our culture. Too many people are subscribing to the elite's smoke-and-mirrors game. Severing us from reality, the ruling elite hide their collusion in the predatory seizure of power and wealth.

Psychological warfare, or psyops, are most effective when they are closely based on fact. Elites understand this principle and mix truths with misrepresentations to increase the credibility of their storyline. Partial truths deceive, confuse, demoralize, and weaken the masses without firing a single bullet. Psyops can also spread information claiming to be from one source that is actually from another. Words, in the form of propaganda, are stronger than weapons. The ultimate challenge is to achieve submission by winning the hearts and minds of the people through psychological manipulation. Many have already succumbed to the elite's unrelenting psyops. Truth will be revealed by those who intentionally seek it out. Discovering it will expose the deceit of the world's most powerful. The ruling elite recognize the truth as the foremost threat to their dominance.

Choosing not to act is a choice, and a choice with devastating consequences. Albert Einstein said, "The world will not be destroyed by those who do evil, but by those who watch them without doing anything." Morals don't always align with civics. Hiding Jews from torture and potential death was a criminal act during the Holocaust. In the early days of the United States, slavery was legal but freeing them was not. Segregation was lawful in the 1960s while protesting it was criminalized. Legal opioid drugs kill tens of thousands of people each year while safer and less addictive cannabis medicines remain prohibited in many jurisdictions. Sometimes, brave "criminals" expressing civil disobedience are needed to halt immoral and unethical practices that are deemed legal. However hard to obtain and no matter the cost, we must search for and divulge truth.

The most consequential war in human history is the silent one being fought between elites and common people. Central to their plan is the destabilization of independent nations to seize world governance by global dictate. Behind it all is something more sinister and evil. Success for us in this shadow war depends on embracing the good in humanity and developing the fifteen character traits mentioned in this book. A person with good character traits is armed to choose what is morally and ethically right. We must emphasize the development of these positive character traits to stop the recurring domination of the minority over the majority. Nelson Mandela said, "When a man is denied the right to live the life he believes in, he has no choice but to become an outlaw." There may come a time when you need to become an outlaw and take appropriate action to secure a free future.

Humans are inherently good with unlimited potential. We must step outside the programming and false reality we have let dominate our life and direct our actions to restore goodness in humanity. Plan your escape from the indoctrination and reunite with the good within you. Unleash your unlimited potential. Be a bright beacon of hope. Help others see the possibilities by your example. Create the world you and our posterity want to live in by your actions. Your value is not determined by worldly achievements, awards received, or even success. It is determined by your willingness to serve and love your fellow man and positively impact the lives of others. Let the way you live your life define who you are. Every time you stand up for what you believe in, you provide an example for others to follow, which may lead to another person's escape from the elite's programming. Live a life of liberty. Rise from the ashes because you have lost, but you are not defeated. You have failed, but you are not a failure. Regain your humanity.

> One need not destroy one's enemy. One need only destroy his willingness to engage.
>
> —Sun Tzu

REFERENCES

[1] Hamlin JK, Wynn K, Bloom P. Social evaluation by preverbal infants. *Nature*. 2007 Nov 22;450:557-9.

[2] Milgram S. Obedience to Authority: An Experimental View. Reprint edition. June 30, 2009. Harper Perennial Modern Classics: New York.

[3] Burger J. The Milgram Experiment. Available at: https://group2miligramexperiment.weebly.com/jerry-burger.html. Accessed February 20, 2021.

[4] Barron, James (July 25, 1991). Male Fortress Falls at Yale: Bonesmen to Admit Women. Available at: https://www.nytimes.com/1991/07/25/nyregion/male-fortress-falls-at-yale-bonesmen-to-admit-women.html. Accessed February 25, 2021.

[5] Algedi M (November 23, 2017). Meet the Elite: Father of Mainstream Media, Skull and Bones Member Henry Luce. Available at: https://www.activistpost.com/2017/11/meet-elite-father-mainstream-media-skull-bones-member-henry-luce.html. Accessed February 25, 2021.

[6] Gilens M, Page BI. Testing Theories of American Politics: Elites, Interest Groups, and Average Citizens. *Perspectives Politics*. 2014 Sep;12(3):564-81.

[7] Townhall.com. Available at: https://townhall.com/columnists/johnhawkins/2014/10/25/everything-millennials-need-to-know-about-politics-and-economics-in-25-quotes-n1909779. Accessed February 25, 2021.

[8] Abbasi K. Covid-19: politicisation, "corruption," and suppression of science. *BMJ*. 2020;371:m4425.

[9] EIA. US Energy Information Administration. Fossil fuels have made up at least 80% of US fuel mix since 1900. Available at: https://www.eia.gov/todayinenergy/detail.php?id=21912. Accessed February 25, 2021.

[10] Committee for a Responsible Federal Budget. COVID Relief Bill Losing Focus as Details Emerge. Available at: https://www.crfb.org/press-releases/covid-relief-bill-losing-focus. Accessed March 19, 2021.

[11] AllSides Media. Available at: https://www.allsides.com/media-bias/media-bias-chart. Accessed March 19, 2021.

[12] Bernstein C. The CIA and the Media. Available at: http://www.carlbernstein.com/magazine_cia_and_media.php. Accessed February 26, 2021.

[13] Central Intelligence Agency. National Security Association. Family Jewels. Available at: https://nsarchive2.gwu.edu//NSAEBB/NSAEBB222/family_jewels_full.pdf. Accessed February 26, 2021.

[14] School History. Operation Mockingbird. Available at: https://schoolhistory.co.uk/notes/operation-mockingbird/. Accessed February 26, 2021.

[15] History.com. Nofil B. The CIA's Appalling Human Experiments with Mind Control. Available at: https://www.history.com/mkultra-operation-midnight-climax-cia-lsd-experiments. Accessed February 26, 2021.

[16] MRC. Soros Spends Over $48 Million Funding Media Organizations. Available at: https://www.mrc.org/commentary/soros-spends-over-48-million-funding-media-organizations. Accessed March 19, 2021.

[17] Columbia Journalism Review. Journalism's Gates keepers. Available at: https://www.cjr.org/criticism/gates-foundation-journalism-funding.php. Accessed March 19, 2021.

[18] Realclimatescience.com. Real Climate Science. Accessed March 4, 2021. Available at: https://realclimatescience.com/1970s-global-cooling-scare/.

[19] Realclimatescience.com. Real Climate Science. Accessed March 4, 2021. Available at: https://realclimatescience.com/1970s-global-cooling-scare/.

[20] Associated Press. U.N. Predicts Disaster if Global Warming Not Checked. Available at: https://apnews.com/article/bd45c372caf118ec99964ea547880cd0. Accessed March 21, 2021.

[21] BBC. PM warns of climate 'catastrophe'. Available at: http://news.bbc.co.uk/2/hi/uk_news/8313672.stm. Accessed March 21, 2021.

[22] Dr. John Coleman: The Tavistock Institute of Human Relations: Shaping the Moral, Spiritual, Cultural, Political and

Economic Decline of the United States of America. Omni Publications 1999.

[23] William Engdahl: A Century of War - Anglo-American Oil Politics and the New World Order.
p 35; Pluto Press 2004.

[24] Jim Marrs. Rule by Secrecy: The Hidden History That Connects the Trilateral Commission, the Freemasons, and the Great Pyramids. William Morrow Paperbacks 2001.

[25] Brigadier General Smedley G Butler. War is Racket. Feral House 2003.

[26] Nasar S. US Trade Benefits From War. The New York Times. The New York Times, 12 Mar 1991. Accessed March 5, 2021. Available at: http://www.nytimes.com/1991/03/13/business/us-trade-benefits-from-war.html.

[27] Publicintellifence.net. Operation Northwoods. Available at: https://publicintelligence.net/operation-northwoods/. Accessed April 1, 2021.

[28] Dr. John Coleman: Diplomacy by Deception - An Account of the Treasonous Conduct of the Governments of Britain and the United States. Bridger House Publications 1993.

[29] The Political Insider. Obama Added 11 Million to Food Stamps – Trump Has Already Removed 1.5 Million. Available at: https://thepoliticalinsider.com/trump-obama-food-stamps/. Accessed March 8, 2021.

[30] Northwestern, Institute for Policy Research. What Drives Native American Poverty? Sociologist Beth Redbird's research points to job loss, not education, as a key driver. Available at: https://www.ipr.northwestern.edu/news/2020/redbird-what-drives-native-american-poverty.html. Accessed March 24, 2021.

[31] PERC. Un-American Reservations. Available at: https://www.perc.org/2011/02/24/un-american-reservations/. Accessed March 24, 2021.

[32] bls.gov. Labor force characteristics by race and ethnicity, 2017. Available at: https://www.bls.gov/opub/reports/race-and-ethnicity/2017/home.htm. Accessed March 24, 2021.

[33] Anderson TL. Sovereign Nations or Reservations? An Economic History of American Indians. San Francisco: Pacific Research Institute for Public Policy, 1995.

[34] The Heritage Foundation. How Welfare Undermines Marriage and What to Do About It. Available at: https://www.heritage.org/welfare/report/how-welfare-undermines-marriage-and-what-do-about-it. Accessed March 8, 2021.

[35] The Heritage Foundation. How Welfare Undermines Marriage and What to Do About It. Available at: https://www.heritage.org/welfare/report/how-welfare-undermines-marriage-and-what-do-about-it. Accessed March 8, 2021.

[36] The Heritage Foundation. How Welfare Undermines Marriage and What to Do About It. Available at: https://www.heritage.org/welfare/report/how-welfare-undermines-marriage-and-what-do-about-it. Accessed March 8, 2021.

[37] Modern Gentlemen. 20 Statistics on Fatherless Homes and the Importance of Dads. Available at: https://moderngentlemen.net/statistics-on-fatherless-homes/. Accessed March 8, 2021.

[38] United Families International. Fatherlessness, Poverty and Crime. Available at: https://www.unitedfamilies.org/child-development/fatherlessness-poverty-and-crime/. Accessed March 8, 2021.

[39] Mathur A, Brookings Institution Social Mobility Memo. Families Are the Real Issue for Opportunity, Not Inequality. Available at: https://www.brookings.edu/blog/social-mobility-memos/2015/05/26/families-are-the-real-issue-for-opportunity-not-inequality/. Accessed February 28, 2021.

[40] Recotor R, The Heritage Foundation. Role of Parental Work in Child Poverty. Available at: https://www.heritage.org/poverty-and-inequality/report/role-parental-work-child-poverty. Accessed March 31, 2021.

[41] Life Is Beautiful. 36 Shocking Statistics in Fatherless Homes. Available at: https://lifeisbeautiful.org/statistics-on-fatherless-homes/. Accessed March 22, 2021.

[42] Life Is Beautiful. 36 Shocking Statistics in Fatherless Homes. Available at: https://lifeisbeautiful.org/statistics-on-fatherless-homes/. Accessed March 22, 2021.

[43] The Heritage Foundation. How Welfare Undermines Marriage and What to Do About It. Available at: https://www.heritage.org/welfare/report/how-welfare-undermines-marriage-and-what-do-about-it. Accessed March 8, 2021.

[44] Life Is Beautiful. 36 Shocking Statistics in Fatherless Homes. Available at: https://lifeisbeautiful.org/statistics-on-fatherless-homes/. Accessed March 22, 2021.

[45] Stanford News. Zinn's influential history textbook has problems, says Stanford education expert. Available at: https://news.stanford.edu/news/2012/december/wineburg-historiography-zinn-122012.html. Accessed March 8, 2021.

[46] da Silva C. US Schools Have Openly Taught the 1619 Project for Months. Available at: https://www.newsweek.com/u-s-schools-have-openly-taught-1619-project-months-1530138. Accessed March 11, 2021.

[47] Available at: https://www.k12.wa.us/sites/default/files/public/socialstudies/pubdocs/Math%20SDS%20ES%20Framework.pdf. Accessed March 8, 2021.

[48] Nbcnews.com. California's new sex ed guidelines encourage teachers to talk to students about gender identity, masturbation. Available at: https://www.nbcnews.com/news/education/california-s-new-sex-ed-guidelines-encourage-teachers-talk-students-n1003596. Accessed March 8, 2021.

[49] Cambridge Public Schools. Whiteness, Privilege, and Bias. Available at: https://www.cpsd.us/cms/one.aspx?portalId=3042869&pageId=69206927. Accessed March 8, 2021.

[50] Available at: http://k12schoolsdata.s3.amazonaws.com/static/docs/77159bb8-c442-4872-b744-4db3d9e96a8c.pdf. Accessed March 8, 2021.

[51] Investopedia. The Panama Papers: What You Should Know. Available at: https://www.investopedia.com/terms/p/panama-papers.asp. Accessed March 8, 2021.

[52] Jenkins T. The CIA in Hollywood. University of Texas Press 2012.

[53] Judicial Watch. CIA IG report 081315. Available at: https://www.judicialwatch.org/documents/cia-ig-report-081315-2/. Accessed March 8, 2021.

[54] Doron M, Gelman J. Confidential: The Life of Secret Agent Turned Hollywood Tycoon Arnon Milchan. Gefen Books 2011.

[55] BBC News. Hollywood producer Arnon Milchan says he spied for Israel. Available at: https://www.bbc.com/news/world-us-canada-25108559. Accessed March 8, 2021.

[56] Farkas J, Neumayer C. Disguised propaganda from digital to social media. *Second International Handbook of Internet Research*. 2019 Oct:707-23.

[57] Harvard Kennedy School. Pandemics & propaganda: How Chinese state media creates and propagates CCP coronavirus narratives. Available at: https://misinforeview.hks.harvard.edu/article/pandemics-propaganda-how-chinese-state-media-creates-and-propagates-ccp-coronavirus-narratives/. Accessed March 9, 2021.

[58] Baker L. In International Encyclopedia of Education (Third Edition), 2010.

[59] Wade C. Using writing to develop and assess critical thinking. *Teaching Psych*. 1995;22(1):24-28.

[60] Mahmoud NE, Kamel S, Hamza TS. The relationship between tolerance of ambiguity and creativity in architectural design studio. *Creativity Studies*. 2020 Mar;13(1):179-98.

[61] Moran J. UCLA Newsroom. Pause, reflect and give thanks: the power of gratitude during the holidays. Available at: https://newsroom.ucla.edu/stories/gratitude-249167. Accessed March 9, 2021.

[62] Zahn R, Moll J, Paiva M, et al. The Neural Basis of Human Social Values: Evidence from Functional MRI. *Cereb Cortex*. 2009 Feb;19(2):276–283.

[63] Wood AM, Joseph S, Maltby J. Gratitude uniquely predicts satisfaction with life: Incremental validity above the domains and facets of the five factor model. *Personality Individual Diff*. 2008;45:49–54.

[64] Wood AM, Joseph S, Maltby J. Gratitude predicts psychological well-being above the big five facets. *Personality Individual Diff*. 2009;46:443-7.

[65] Dickens L, DeSteno D. The grateful are patient: Heightened daily gratitude is associated with attenuated temporal discounting. *Emotion*. 2016;16(4):421-5.

[66] Nguyen SP, Gordon CL. The Relationship Between Gratitude and Happiness in Young Children. *J Happiness Studies*. 2020;21:2773-87.

[67] Froh JJ, Yurkewicz C, Kashdan TB. Gratitude and subjective well-being in early adolescence: Examining gender differences. *J Adolescence*. 2009 Jun;23(3):633-50.

[68] Youssef A-JS, Froh JJ, Muller ME, et al. Measuring Gratitude in Youth: Assessing the Psychometric Properties of Adult Gratitude Scales in Children and Adolescents. *Psychological Assessment*. 2011;23(2):311-324.

[69] Kubacka KE, Finkenauer C, Rusbult CE. Maintaining Close Relationships: Gratitude as a Motivator and a Detector of Maintenance Behavior. *Pers Soc Psychol Bull*. 2011 Oct;37(10):1362-75.

[70] Dunn JR, Schweitzer ME. Feeling and Believing: The Influence of Emotion on Trust. *J Personality Social Psych*. 2005 May;88(5):736-48.

[71] Barton AW, Futris TG, Nielsen RB. Linking financial distress to marital quality: The intermediary roles of demand/withdraw and spousal gratitude expressions. *Personal Relationships*. 2015Sep;22(3):536-49.

[72] Algoe SB, Haidt J, Gable SL. Beyond reciprocity: Gratitude and relationships in everyday life. *Emotion*. 2008;8(3):425-9.

[73] Yu H, Cai Q, Shen B, et al. Neural Substrates and Social Consequences of Interpersonal Gratitude: Intention Matters. *Emotion*. 2017 Jun;17(4):589-601.

[74] Emmons RA, McCullough ME. Counting blessings versus burdens: an experimental investigation of gratitude and subjective well-being in daily life. *J Pers Soc Psychol*. 2003 Feb;84(2):377-89.

[75] Wood AM, Joseph S, Lloyd J, et al. Gratitude influences sleep through the mechanism of pre-sleep cognitions. *J Psychosom Res*. 2009 Jan;66(1):43-8.

[76] Digdon N, Koble A. Effects of Constructive Worry, Imagery Distraction, and Gratitude Interventions on Sleep Quality: A Pilot Trial. *App Psychology: Health Well-being*. 2011 Jul;3(2):193-206.

[77] Rash JA, Matsuba MK, Prkachin KM. Gratitude and Well-Being: Who Benefits the Most from a Gratitude Intervention? *App Psychology: Health Well-being.* 2011;3(3):350-69.

[78] Redwine L, Henry BL, Pung MA, et al. A pilot randomized study of a gratitude journaling intervention on HRV and inflammatory biomarkers in Stage B heart failure patients. *Psychosom Med.* 2016;78(6):667-76.

[79] Hill PL, Allemand M, Roberts BW. Examining the Pathways between Gratitude and Self-Rated Physical Health across Adulthood. *Pers Individ Dif.* 2013 Jan;54(1):92–96.

[80] Thompson SP. Worried about Thanksgiving overeating? Giving thanks before meals helps weight control, health. Available at: https://mycitylife.ca/people/health/worried-about-thanksgiving-overeating-giving-thanks-before-meals-helps-weight-control-health/. Accessed March 10, 2021.

[81] Sonnby–Borgström M. Automatic mimicry reactions as related to differences in emotional empathy. *Scandinavian J Psych.* 2002;43:433–443.

[82] O'Doherty J, Winston J, Critchley H, et al. Beauty in a smile: the role of medial orbitofrontal cortex in facial attractiveness. *Neuropsychologia.* 2003;41:147–155.

[83] YaleNews. Women smile more than men, but differences disappear when they are in the same role, Yale researcher finds. Available at: https://news.yale.edu/2003/03/18/women-smile-more-men-differences-disappear-when-they-are-same-role-yale-researcher-finds. Accessed March 12, 2021.

[84] Lane RD. Neural correlates of conscious emotional experience. 2000. In R.D. Lane & L. Nadel (Eds.), Cognitive neuroscience of emotion (pp. 345–370). New York: Oxford University Press.

[85] Seaward BL. Managing Stress: Principles and Strategies for Health and Well-Being. Sudbury, Massachussets: Jones and Bartlett; 2009:258.

[86] Bashir H, Bhat S. Effects of Social Media on Mental Health: A Review. *Int J Indian Psych.* 2015 Dec;4(3):125-31.

[87] Anderson CA, Bushman BJ, Bartholow BD, et al. Screen Violence and Youth Behavior. *Pediatrics.* 2017 Nov;140(Suppl 2):S142-S147.

[88] Bilgram Z, McLaughlin L, Milanaik R, et al. Health implications of new-age technologies: a systematic review. *Minerva Pediatr*. 2017 Aug;69(4):348-367.

[89] Anderson CA, Carnagey NL, Eubanks J. Exposure to violent media: The effects of songs with violent lyrics on aggressive thoughts and feelings. *J Personality Social Psych*. 2003;84(5):960.

[90] Oliver MB, Hatmann T, Woolley JK. Elevation in Response to Entertainment Portrayals of Moral Virtue. *Human Communication Res*. 2012 Jul;38(3):360-78.

[91] Aquino K, McFerran B, Laven M. Moral identity and the experience of moral elevation in response to acts of uncommon goodness. *J Pers Soc Psychol*. 2011 Apr;100(4):703-18.

[92] Janicke SH, Oliver MB. The relationship between elevation, connectedness, and compassionate love in meaningful films. *Psych Pop Media Culture*. 2017;6(3):274-89.

[93] Stanford University. New studies of human brains show stress may shrink neurons. Available at: https://news.stanford.edu/pr/96/960814shrnkgbrain.html. Accessed March 12, 2021.

[94] Bueno VF, Kozasa EH, da Silva MA, et al. Mindfulness Meditation Improves Mood, Quality of Life, and Attention in Adults with Attention Deficit Hyperactivity Disorder. *Biomed Res Int*. 2015;2015:962857.

[95] Hofmann SG, Sawyer AT, Witt AA, et al. The Effect of Mindfulness-Based Therapy on Anxiety and Depression: A Meta-Analytic Review. *J Consult Clin Psychol*. 2010 Apr;78(2):169–183.

[96] Hoge EA, Bui E, Marques L, et al. Randomized Controlled Trial of Mindfulness Meditation for Generalized Anxiety Disorder: Effects on Anxiety and Stress Reactivity. *J Clin Psychiatry*. 2013 Aug;74(8):786–792.

[97] Wu R, Liu LL, Zhu H, et al. Brief Mindfulness Meditation Improves Emotion Processing. *Front Neurosci*. 2019;13:1074.

[98] Gard T, Holzel BK, Lazar SW. The potential effects of meditation on age-related cognitive decline: a systematic review. *Ann N Y Acad Sci*. 2014 Jan;1307:89-103.

[99] Hilton L, Hempel S, Ewing BA, et al. Mindfulness Meditation for Chronic Pain: Systematic Review and Meta-analysis. *Ann Behav Med.* 2017;51(2):199–213.

[100] Creswell JD, Myers HF, Cole SW, et al. Mindfulness meditation training effects on CD4+ T lymphocytes in HIV-1 infected adults: a small randomized controlled trial. *Brain Behav Immun.* 2009 Feb;23(2):184-8.

[101] Younge JO, Wery MF, Gotink RA, et al. Web-Based Mindfulness Intervention in Heart Disease: A Randomized Controlled Trial. *PLoS One.* 2015 Dec 7;10(12):e0143843.

[102] Carlson LE. Mindfulness-Based Interventions for Physical Conditions: A Narrative Review Evaluating Levels of Evidence. *ISRN Psychiatry.* 2012; 2012: 651583.

[103] Ok E, Qian Y, Strejcek B, et al. Signaling virtuous victimhood as indicators of Dark Triad personalities. *J Personality Social Psych.* 2020 Jul 2. Online ahead of print.

[104] Fredrickson BL. The broaden-and-build theory of positive emotions. *Phil Trans R Soc Lond B.* 2004;359:1367-77.

[105] DuBois CM, Lopez OV, Beale EE, et al. Relationships between positive psychological constructs and health outcomes in patients with cardiovascular disease: a systematic review. *Int J Cardiol.* 2015 Sep 15; 195: 265–280.

[106] Kubzansky LD, Huffman JC, Boehm JK, et al. Positive Psychological Well-Being and Cardiovascular Disease: JACC Health Promotion Series. *J Am College Cardiology.* 2018 sep;72(12):1382-96.

[107] Cameron K, Mora C, Leutscher T, et al. Effects of Positive Practices on Organizational Effectiveness. *J Appl Behavior Sci.* 2011;47(3).

[108] The Guardian. The path to happiness: it is better to give than receive. Available at: https://www.theguardian.com/science/2008/mar/21/medicalresearch.usa. Accessed March 15, 2021.

[109] Monson TS. Three Goals to Guide You. Available at. https://www.churchofjesuschrist.org/study/general-conference/2007/10/three-goals-to-guide-you?lang=eng. Accessed March 15, 2021.

[110] Baumeister RF, Vohs KD, Aaker J, et al. Some Key Differences between a Happy Life and a Meaningful Life. *J Positive Psych*. 2013;8(6):505-16.

[111] Dossey L. The Helper's High. *Explore*. 2018 Nov;14(6):393-9.

[112] Carnegie Mellon University. Press Release: Volunteering Reduces Risk of Hypertension In Older Adults, Carnegie Mellon Research Shows. Available at: https://www.cmu.edu/news/stories/archives/2013/june/june13_volunteeringhypertension.html/. Accessed March 15, 2021.

[113] US Centers for Disease Control and Prevention. Hypertension Prevalence Among Adults Aged 18 and Over: United States, 2017–2018. Available at: https://www.cdc.gov/nchs/products/databriefs/db364.htm. Accessed March 15, 2021.

[114] Kim ES, Whillians AV, Lee MT, et al. Volunteering and Subsequent Health and Well-Being in Older Adults: An Outcome-Wide Longitudinal Approach. *Am J Prevent Med*. 2020 Aug;59(2):176-86.

[115] Eskreis-Winkler L, Fishbach A, Duckworth AL. Dear Abby: Should I Give Advice or Receive It? *Psychol Sci*. 2018 Nov; 29(11):1797–1806.

[116] Bible, King James Version. Matthew 22:36-40.

[117] Regier J, Pardue M. The effects of marriage on health: A synthesis of recent research evidence. Research Brief. Available at: https://aspe.hhs.gov/report/effects-marriage-health-synthesis-recent-research-evidence-research-brief. Accessed March 15, 2021.

[118] Arnon A, Fisher H, Mashek DJ, et al. Reward, Motivation, and Emotion Systems Associated With Early-Stage Intense Romantic Love. *J Neurophysiol*. 2005;94:327–337.

[119] Jones B. Is There Something Unique about Marriage? The Relative Impact of Marital Status, Relationship Quality, and Network Social Support on Ambulatory Blood Pressure and Mental Health. *Ann Behav Med*. 2008 Apr;35(2):239-44.

[120] Cohen S, Doyle WJ, Turner RB, et al. Emotional style and susceptibility to the common cold. *Psychosom Med*. Jul-Aug 2003;65(4):652-7.

[121] Kiecolt-Glaser JK, Loving TJ, Stowell JR, et al. Hostile Marital Interactions, Proinflammatory Cytokine Production, and Wound Healing. *Arch Gen Psychiatry*. 2005;62(12):1377–1384.

[122] Kaplan RM, Kronick RG. Marital status and longevity in the United States population. *J Epidemiol Comm Health.* 2006;60(9):760-5.

[123] WebMD, Boyles S. For Happiness, Seek Family, Not Fortune. Available at: https://www.webmd.com/balance/news/20080619/for-happiness-seek-family-not-fortune. Accessed March 15, 2021.

[124] Singer T, Klimecki OM. Empathy and Compassion. *Curr Biol.* 2014;24:875-878.

[125] Silani G, Lamm C, Ruff C, et al. Right Supramarginal Gyrus Is Crucial to Overcome Emotional Egocentricity Bias in Social Judgments. *J Neurosci.* 2013;33(39):15466.

[126] Mcdonald NM, Messinger DS. The development of empathy: How, when, and why. Available at: https://www.researchgate.net/publication/267426505_The_Development_of_Empathy_How_When_and_Why. Accessed March 15, 2021.

[127] Mestre MV, Samper P, Frias MD, et al. Are women more empathetic than men? A longitudinal study in adolescence. *Span J Psychol.* 2009 May;12(1):76-83.

[128] CBS Denver. Colorado Officer Donates Organ To Young Stranger, Then Helps Pay The Medical Bill. Available at: https://denver.cbslocal.com/2019/12/20/carolyn-becker-clyde-hoffman-alagilles-syndrome-colorado-officer-donates-organ-helps-pay-medical-bill/. Accessed March 22, 2021.

[129] Redi N. Why diversity without inclusion is tokenism. Available at: linkedin.com/pulse/why-diversity-without-inclusion-tokenism-nova-reid/. Accessed March 16, 2021.

[130] National Center for Education Statistics. Race/ethnicity of college faculty. Available at: https://nces.ed.gov/fastfacts/display.asp?id=61. Accessed April 7, 2021.

[131] Langbert M, Quain AJ, Klein DB. Faculty Voter Registration in Economics, History, Journalism, Law, and Psychology. Available at: https://econjwatch.org/articles/faculty-voter-registration-in-economics-history-journalism-communications-law-and-psychology. Accessed April 7, 2021.

[132] U.S. Census Bureau. Quick Facts, Atlanta city, Georgia. Available at: https://www.census.gov/quickfacts/fact/table/atlantacitygeorgia/PST045219. Accessed April 7, 2021.

[133] U.S. Census Bureau. Quick Facts, Denver County, Colorado. Available at: https://www.census.gov/quickfacts/denvercountycolorado. Accessed April 7, 2021.

[134] Edgar L, newsbreak.com. Poll: Nearly Three-Fourths Of Americans Want Voter-ID Laws. Available at: https://www.newsbreak.com/news/2197277974028/poll-nearly-three-fourths-of-americans-want-voter-id-laws. Accessed April 7, 2021.

[135] Civitas UK. Christianophobia. Available at: http://www.civitas.org.uk/pdf/Shortt_Christianophobia.pdf. Accessed March 22, 2021.

[136] Genesis 37:20.

[137] History.com. 8 Things You May Not Know About Hammurabi's Code. Available at: https://www.history.com/news/8-things-you-may-not-know-about-hammurabis-code. Accessed March 24, 2021.

[138] Wilkin S. A History of Slavery Sparta and Helot. 2019 Dec. Available at: https://www.researchgate.net/publication/337843528_A_History_of_Slavery_Sparta_and_Helot. Accessed March 24, 2021.

[139] Charlseworth TES, Bananji MR. Patterns of Implicit and Explicit Attitudes: I. Long-Term Change and Stability From 2007 to 2016. *Assoc Psych Sci*. 2019;30(2):174-92.

[140] Hopkins DJ, Washington S. The Rise of Trump, the Fall of Prejudice? Tracking White Americans' Racial Attitudes 2008-2018 via a Panel Survey. Available at: https://papers.ssrn.com/sol3/papers.cfm?abstract_id=3378076. Accessed March 30, 2021.

[141] Cracked.com. 5 Studies That Prove Racism Is Still Way Worse Than We Think. Available at: https://www.cracked.com/article_21822_5-studies-that-prove-racism-still-way-worse-than-we-think.html. Accessed March 30, 2021.

[142] Business Insider. 26 simple charts to show friends and family who aren't convinced racism is still a problem in America. Available at: https://www.businessinsider.com/us-systemic-racism-in-charts-graphs-data-2020-6?op=1. Accessed March 30, 2021.

[143] Mucha R. When diversity efforts backfire: Advice to avoid legal trouble. Available at: https://www.hrmorning.com/articles/when-diversity-efforts-backfire-advice-to-avoid-legal-trouble/. Accessed March 31, 2021.

[144] MSN. Coca-Cola promotes guidelines to 'be less white'. Available at: https://www.msn.com/en-us/lifestyle/lifestyle-buzz/coca-cola-promotes-guidelines-to-be-less-white/ar-BB1dUFeV. Accessed March 31, 2021.

[145] US Sentencing Commission. Report on the Continuing Impact of United States v. Booker on Federal Sentencing. Available at: https://www.ussc.gov/sites/default/files/pdf/news/congressional-testimony-and-reports/booker-reports/2012-booker/Part_A.pdf#page=55. Accessed March 22, 2021.

[146] The Hamilton Project. The Historical Role of Race and Policy for Regional Inequality. Available at: https://www.hamiltonproject.org/papers/the_historical_role_of_race_and_policy_for_regional_inequality. Accessed March 23, 2021.

[147] National Center for Education Statistics. School Composition and the Black-White Achievement Gap. Available at: https://nces.ed.gov/pubsearch/pubsinfo.asp?pubid=2015018. Accessed March 24, 2021.

[148] National Center for Education Statistics. SAT Scores. Available at: https://nces.ed.gov/fastfacts/display.asp?id=171. Accessed March 24, 2021.

[149] Selfgrowth.com. Why Do Black Americans Fail in School? Available at: https://www.selfgrowth.com/articles/why-do-black-americans-fail-in-school/. Accessed March 24, 2021.

[150] United States Census Bureau. Inequalities Persist Despite Decline in Poverty For All Major Race and Hispanic Origin Groups. https://www.census.gov/library/stories/2020/09/poverty-rates-for-blacks-and-hispanics-reached-historic-lows-in-2019.html. Accessed March 23, 2021.

[151] The Brookings Institution. Three Simple Rules Poor Teens Should Follow to Join the Middle Class. Available at: https://www.brookings.edu/opinions/three-simple-rules-poor-teens-should-follow-to-join-the-middle-class/. Accessed March 23, 2021.

[152] Newsweek. Why Are Black Americans at Greater Risk of Being Poor? Available at: https://www.newsweek.com/why-are-black-americans-greater-risk-being-poor-361543. Accessed March 23, 2021.

[153] Leonhardt D. The Black-White Wage Gap Is as Big as It Was in 1950. Available at: https://www.nytimes.com/2020/06/25/opinion/sunday/race-wage-gap.html. Accessed February 28, 2021.

[154] O'Neill JE and O'Neill DM. The Declining Importance of Race and Gender in the Labor Market: The Role of Employment Discrimination Policies. Washington: AEI Press, 2012.

[155] Rector R, Johnson KA, Fagan PF. Understanding Differences in Black and White Child Poverty Rates," Heritage Foundation Center for Data Analysis Report No. Available at: https://www.heritage.org/welfare/report/understanding-differences-black-and-white-child-poverty-rates. Accessed February 28, 2021.

[156] Haskins R, Pew Charitable Trusts, Economic Mobility Initiative. Education and Economic Mobility. Available at: https://www.brookings.edu/wp-content/uploads/2016/07/02_economic_mobility_sawhill_ch8.pdf. Accessed March 31, 2021.

[157] US Census Bureau. Income and Poverty in the United States: 2018. Available at: https://www.census.gov/library/publications/2019/demo/p60-266.html. Accessed March 24, 2021.

[158] Owens BP, Hekman DR. Modeling How to Grow: An Inductive Examination of Humble Leader Behaviors, Contingencies, and Outcomes. *Academy Manag J.* 2012 Apr 30;55(4):787-818

[159] Ou AY, Waldman DA, Peterson SJ. Do Humble CEOs Matter? An Examination of CEO Humility and Firm Outcomes. *J Manag.* 2015 Sep;44(3):1-27.

[160] Johnson MK, Rowatt WC, Petrini L. A new trait on the market: Honesty–Humility as a unique predictor of job performance ratings. *Personality Ind Diff.* 2011 Apr;50(6):857-62.

[161] Rowatt WC, Powers C, Targhetta V, et al. Development and initial validation of an implicit measure of humility relative to arrogance. *J Pos Psych.* 2006;1(4):198-211.

[162] Davis DE, Worthington Jr AL, Hook JN, et al. Humility and the Development and Repair of Social Bonds: Two Longitudinal Studies. *Self Identity*. 2013;13(1):58-77.

[163] Wenzheng L, Humility shaping social judgments: The effect of humility of stereotyping mediated by egalitarian beliefs. *PhD Theses (Open)*. Available at: https://scholarbank.nus.edu.sg/handle/10635/166281. Accessed March 17, 2021.

[164] LaBouff JP. Rowatt WC, Johnson MK, et al. Humble persons are more helpful than less humble persons: Evidence from three studies. *J Pos Psych*. 2012;7(1):16-29.

[165] Seligman MEP. The Hope Circuit: A Psychologist's Journey from Helplessness to Optimism. PublicAffairs, 2018.

[166] Nicholls AR, Polman RCJ, Levy AR, et al. Mental toughness, optimism, pessimism, and coping among athletes. *Person Ind Diff*. 2008 Apr;44(5):1182-92.

[167] Rahimipour M, Shahgholian N, Yazdani M. Effect of hope therapy on depression, anxiety, and stress among the patients undergoing hemodialysis. *Iran J Nurs Midwifery Res*. Nov-Dec 2015;20(6):694-9.

[168] Sadeghi H, Ebrahimi L, Vatandoust L. Effectiveness of Hope Therapy Protocol on Depression and Hope in Amphetamine Users. *Int J High Risk Behav Addict*. 2015 Dec;4(4):e21905.

[169] Stevens E, Guerrero M, Green A, et al. Relationship of hope, sense of community, and quality of life. *J Community Psychol*. 2018 Jul;46(5):567–574.

[170] Gallagher MW, Long LJ, Richardson A, et al. Examining Hope as a Transdiagnostic Mechanism of Change Across Anxiety Disorders and CBT Treatment Protocols. *Behav Ther*. 2020 Jan;51(1):190-202.

[171] Srivastava S, McGonigal KM, Richaards JM, et al. Optimism in close relationships: How seeing things in a positive light makes them so. *J Person Soc Psych*. 2006 Jul;91(1):143-53.

[172] Bressler M, Nressler L, Bressler M. The role and relationship of hope, optimism, and goal setting in achieving academic success: A study of students enrolled in online accounting. *Academy Ed Lead J*. 2010 Nov;14(4):37-48.

[173] Gomez-Molinero R, Zayas A, Ruiz-Gonzalez P, et al. Optimism and resilience among university students. *Int J Develop Ed Psych*. 2018;1(1):147-54.

[174] Singh I, Jha A. Anxiety, Optimism and Academic Achievement among Students of Private Medical and Engineering Colleges: A Comparative Study. *J Ed Devel Psych*. 2013;3(1):222-33.

[175] Cankaya EM. The Role of Hope and Optimism on Graduate Students' Academic Performance, Physical Health and Well-Being. Available at: https://oaktrust.library.tamu.edu/bitstream/handle/1969.1/157742/CANKAYA-DISSERTATION-2016.pdf?sequence=1&isAllowed=y. Accessed March 17, 2021.

[176] Long KNG, Kim ES, Chen Y, et al. The role of Hope in subsequent health and well-being for older adults: An outcome-wide longitudinal approach. *Global Epidemiol*. 2020 Nov;2:100018.

[177] Lee LO, James P, Zevon ES, et al. Optimism is associated with exceptional longevity in 2 epidemiologic cohorts of men and women. *Proc Natl Acad Sci U S A*. 2019 Sep 10;116(37):18357-18362.

[178] Ramirez-Maestre C, Esteve R, Lopez AE. The role of optimism and pessimism in chronic pain patients adjustment. *Span J Psychol*. 2012 Mar;15(1):286-94.

[179] Katsimigod AM, O'Beirne S, Harmon D. Hope and chronic pain—a systematic review. *Irish J Med Sci*. 2021;190:307-312.

[180] Segerstrom SC, Taylor SE, Kemeny ME, et al. Optimism Is Associated With Mood, Coping, and Immune Change in Response to Stress. *J Personal Social Psych*. 1998;74(6):1646-55.

[181] vanOyen-Witvliet C, Richie FJ, Luna LMR, et al. Gratitude Predicts Hope and Happiness: A Two study Assessment of Traits and States. *J Pos Psych*. 2018. Available at: https://digitalcommons.hopc.cdu/cgi/viewcontent.cgi?article–2591&context=faculty_publications. Accessed March 17, 2021.

[182] Whittington BL, Scher SJ. Prayer and subjective well-being: An examination of six different types of prayer. *Int J Psych Religion*. 2010 Nov;20(1):59-68.

[183] The Book of Mormon. Moroni 7:45. Available at: https://www.churchofjesuschrist.org/study/scriptures/bofm/moro/7.45?lang=eng#p45. Accessed March 18, 2021.

[184] Mischel W, Ebbesen, EB. Attention In Delay Of Gratification. J Personality Social Psych. 1970;16(2):329–337.

[185] Mischel W, Shoda Y, Rofriguez MI. Delay of gratification in children. *Science*. 1989 May 26;244(4907):933-938.

[186] Ayduk O, Mendoza-Denton R, Mischel W, et al. Regulating the interpersonal self: Strategic self-regulation for coping with rejection sensitivity. *J Personality Social Psych*. 2000;79(5):776-92.

[187] Schlam TR, Wilson NL, Schoda Y, et al. Preschoolers' delay of gratification predicts their body mass 30 years later. *J Pediatrics*. 2013 Jan;162(1):90-93.

[188] Shoda Y, Mischel W, Peake PK. Predicting Adolescent Cognitive and Self-Regulatory Competencies from Preschool Delay of Gratification: Identifying Diagnostic Conditions. *Develop Psych*. 1990;26(6):978-86.

[189] Watts TW, Duncan GJ, Quan H. Revisiting the Marshmallow Test: A Conceptual Replication Investigating Links Between Early Delay of Gratification and Later Outcomes. 2018;29(7):1-92.

[190] Jerath R, Edry JW, Barnes VA, et al. Physiology of long pranayamic breathing: neural respiratory elements may provide a mechanism that explains how slow deep breathing shifts the autonomic nervous system. *Med Hypotheses*. 2006;67(3):566-71.

[191] Yim J. Therapeutic Benefits of Laughter in Mental Health: A Theoretical Review. *Tohoku J Exp Med*. 2016 Jul;239(3):243-9.

[192] Bendavid E, Oh C, Bhattacharya J, et al. Assessing mandatory stay-at-home and business closure effects on the spread of COVID-19. *Eur J Clin Invest*. 2021 Apr;51(4):e13484.

[193] Joffe A. COVID-19: Rethinking the Lockdown Groupthink. *Frontiers Pub Health*. 2021 Feb;9:625778.

[194] CBS News. Suicide claimed more Japanese lives in October than 10 months of COVID. Available at: https://www.cbsnews.com/news/japan-suicide-coronavirus-more-japanese-suicides-in-october-than-total-covid-deaths/. Accessed March 18, 2021.

[195] The Guardian. Billionaires' wealth rises to $10.2 trillion amid Covid crisis. Available at: https://www.theguardian.com/business/2020/oct/07/covid-19-crisis-boosts-the-fortunes-of-worlds-billionaires. Accessed March 18, 2021.

[196] The Guardian. Ten billionaires reap $400bn boost to wealth during pandemic. Available at: https://www.theguardian.com/technology/2020/dec/19/ten-billionaires-reap-400bn-boost-to-wealth-during-pandemic. Accessed March 18, 2021.

[197] Krugman S. Experiments at the Willowbrook State School. *Lancet*. 1971 May 8;1(7706):966-7.

[198] Comfort N. The prisoner as model organism: malaria research at Stateville Penitentiary. *Stud Hist Philos Biol Biomed Sci*. 2009 Sep;40(3):190-203.

[199] CBS News, Mabrey V. A Dark Chapter in Medical History. Available at: https://www.cbsnews.com/news/a-dark-chapter-in-medical-history-09-02-2005/. Accessed April 1, 2021.

[200] Themillenniumreport.com. Illegal Human Experimentation Conducted by the C.I.A. in the United States (Abridged List). Available at: http://themillenniumreport.com/2017/09/illegal-human-experimentation-conducted-by-the-c-i-a-in-the-united-states-abridged-list//. Accessed April 1, 2021.

[201] The Los Angeles Times. CDC Says It Erred in Measles Study. Available at: https://www.latimes.com/archives/la-xpm-1996-06-17-mn-15871-story.html. Accessed April 1, 2021.

[202] Trattato Di Sociologia Generale. Nabu Press.

INDEX

state-controlled media 24
Stateville Penitentiary 177
Stewart, Potter 15
Stimson, Henry 15
Swain, Carol 125
Sweden 92, 171
Syria 49

T
Taft, William Howard 15
taxes 20, 40-41, 122
tokenism 112-114
Trippe, Juan Henry 15
Trump, Donald 49, 117
Tubman, Harriet 158
Tuskegee experiment 173-174
Twain, Mark 81
Tzu, Sun 180

U
Ukraine 43-44
United Kingdom (UK) 11, 18, 19,
        114, 172
United Nations (UN) 26
United States (US) 30, 31, 32, 33,
        34, 36, 38, 44, 77, 78,
        115, 119, 120, 126, 159,
        171, 172, 175, 179
US Constitution 118, 119, 159
US Supreme Court 15, 119

V
Van Gogh, Vincent 104
van Hulst, Johan 91

Vanderbilt, Cornelius 11
von Goethe, Johann Wolfgang 136
victim mentality 75-77
Vietnam 24
virtue signaling 170-171

W
Wade, Carole 50
Wallenberg, Raoul 91
Walsch, Neale Donald 134
war 10, 29-32, 92, 118, 119, 121,
        137, 179
Washington, Booker T. 45
welfare 32-37, 113
Wilde, Oscar 176
Willowbrook State School 174
Wilson, Woodrow 31
Winfrey, Oprah 76
Wood, Douglas 66
World War I 30, 137
World War II 10, 31, 92, 119

Y
Yale University 127
Young, Brigham 82

Z
Zedong, Mao 10
Zuckerberg, Mark 173

www.ingramcontent.com/pod-product-compliance
Lightning Source LLC
Chambersburg PA
CBHW072137270326
41931CB00010B/1787